Horace
Thomas
10-26-01

HOW TO BUILD A MILLION-DOLLAR FORTUNE

Other Books by Tyler G. Hicks
Published by Prima Publishing & Communications

How to Borrow Your Way to Real Estate Riches

How to Start Your Own Business on a Shoe-String and Make Up to $500,000 a Year

How to Get Rich on Other People's Money: Going from Flat Broke to Great Wealth with Creative Financing

HOW TO ORDER:

Quantity discounts are available from Prima Publishing & Communications, Post Office Box 1260HD, Rocklin, CA 95677; telephone (916) 624-5718. On your letterhead include information concerning the intended use of the books and the number of books you wish to purchase.

U.S. Bookstores and Libraries: Please submit all orders to St. Martin's Press, 175 Fifth Avenue, New York, NY 10010; telephone (212) 674-5151.

HOW TO BUILD A MILLION-DOLLAR FORTUNE

*The 14-Day No-Nonsense Program
to Start You on the
Road to Riches*

TYLER G. HICKS

Prima Publishing & Communications
P.O. Box 1260HD
Rocklin, CA 95677
(916) 624-5718

Typography by Col D'var Graphics
Production by Bookman Productions
Jacket design by The Dunlavey Studio

Prima Publishing & Communications
Rocklin, CA

Library of Congress Cataloging-in-Publication Data
Hicks, Tyler Gregory, 1921–
How to build a million-dollar fortune.

Includes index.
1. Investments.   2. Finance, Personal.   I. Title.
HG4521.H565   1989   332.024   88-35737
ISBN 0-914629-81-6

89 90 91 92   RRD   10 9 8 7 6 5 4 3 2 1

Printed in the United States of America

WHAT THIS BOOK DOES FOR YOU

Your mind can make you rich! And this book gives *you* key success action secrets for winning great wealth quickly today. It shows you exactly how to use your mind to make yourself rich—using a simple 14-day success action program to build a million-dollar fortune.

Dealing with thousands of Beginning Wealth Builders (BWBs I call them) the way I do, I see certain actions that can almost guarantee quick wealth success for anyone—including *you*! So you're given step-by-step proven success methods that will help you get rich in any business you like. And *you* can put these methods to work in 14 days, or less. Can anything be faster?

So come along with me—good friend—while you have fun seeing how to:

- Know what you want in life—and get it!
- Visualize your achievements—and watch them come true in your life.
- Plan your great successes—and start moving ahead in just 14 days!
- Take action to succeed—and start being successful today.
- Adopt a Rich Mental Attitude (RMA) and watch your riches grow quickly.
- Build on your early successes to move ahead to your million-dollar fortune.
- Overcome *all* road blocks—blow them away with the greatest of ease!
- Be a results person every day and see your successes grow into your dreams!
- Win people to your cause and get them to help you make your fortune.
- Share your success and prosper richly, helping others build great wealth!

No matter what business or real-estate deal turns you on, you can make it a rich success fast by taking the *right* action.

In this book you are shown exactly how to take that right action to build great personal wealth—quickly and surely. And you'll compress the time needed for your success from years to just days!

To be sure you reach your wealth goals sooner, I'm as close to you as your telephone. You can call me—day or night, weekdays or weekends—and I'll answer your questions. Or I'll act as a sounding board to bounce ideas off, or even consider providing loan money for your deal. So *you* get answers in minutes—instead of in the weeks or months usually taken by conventional lenders. I call this my Loans By Phone service!

And—as an extra service for you—I can provide the names, addresses, and telephone numbers of living, breathing wealth builders who're making their fortunes today. You can:

- Contact directly one or more of these successful people and get firsthand info on what's working for them.
- Or, if you'd prefer, I'll contact these same people and get answers to any questions *you* may have.
- Again, you'll get your answers in just minutes—instead of in the days (or weeks) normally needed.

So this book will get *you* started building great wealth quickly and easily today—using your own skills. It will work for you in any business you pick—anywhere. Just give these practical, sensible, and workable methods 14 days—or less—and you'll be on the road to great wealth.

So let's get started making *you* rich! Remember—you have a steady and dependable friend in your author—Ty Hicks. So turn to Chapter 1 and start getting rich in your own successful business! It's fun, it's rewarding, and you'll never again have to take orders from a surly, nasty boss. Just that thought should be enough to make you want to get rich—using your own mind. Let's start—*now*!

TYLER G. HICKS

CONTENTS

DAY 1

CHAPTER 1

TO BUILD GREAT WEALTH, KNOW WHAT YOU WANT 3

You Get What You Think 3
What Turns You On? 5
Figure Out What You Really Want 6
How Large an Income Do You Need? 8
Five Steps to Your True Drives 10
Go Where Your Interests Push You 11
Pick the Best Way to Build Your Wealth 12
How to Get Your Own Business 13
Understand Financing and Get Money 14
Loan Helps You Can Use 16
Have an Acceptable Purpose For Your Loan 19
Raise Nonrepayable Capital 20
Sell Stock in Your Corporation 21
Use Limited Partners to Get Money 23
Get Hard-Cash Grants 24
Move Ahead to Your Wealth 25

DAY 2

CHAPTER 2

PLAN YOUR SUCCESS—AND WORK YOUR PLAN 29

You Always Need a Plan 29
Good Business Plans Can Make You Millions 30
What Your Business Plan Should Cover 31
How to Start Your Business Plan 33
Doing Your Executive Summary 34
Five Paragraphs to Potential Millions 35

Doing the Rest of Your Plan   39
Why Planning Really Works   45

DAY 3

CHAPTER 3

VISUALIZE YOUR ACHIEVEMENTS— AND ENJOY THEM 51

Use Mental Pictures to Show the Way   51
Keep Your Goals in Front of You Every Day   53
Enjoy Your Goals to Achieve Them   54
See Goals That Put You in Command   55

DAY 4

CHAPTER 4

ADOPT A RICH MENTAL ATTITUDE— AND BANK THE RESULTS 75

So What Is a Rich Mental Attitude?   75
Build a Million-Dollar Fortune on Your RMA   77
How To Combine Your RMA with Business Success   80
Treat Yourself to Riches—USE OPM   81
Other Ways to Use Your RMA   87
Get Money from Friendly Sources   93
Your RMA Will Really Work for You   95

DAY 5

CHAPTER 5

TAKE ACTION TO SUCCEED—AND BUILD GREAT WEALTH 99

The Three Keys to Your Million-Dollar Fortune   99
You Can't Go Wrong by Taking Action   100
Plan the Actions You'll Take   100

Base Your Actions on Your Business Plan   101
All Action Will Pay You   105
Build Your Wealth Using a Simple Umbrella   106
Wealth-Building Actions for Everyone   107
Simple Actions for Over $100,000 a Year   108
Where to Find Millions for Any Business   110
Mine the Home Equity Gold Rush   112
Other Ways to Get Money Through Action   115
Action Does Get and Make Money   116

DAY 6

CHAPTER 6

WIN PEOPLE TO YOUR CAUSE— AND GET ANY NEEDED HELP   121

Thank Goodness for Customers   122
Go the Extra Mile for Every Customer   125
Be Nice to Your Suppliers—It Pays   126
Build Employee Loyalty Every Day   128
Treat Regulators with Respect   129
Get Help from Trade Associations   133
Don't Overlook General Business Groups   133
Get Extra Benefits from Your Business   134
Get Started for Pennies   135
Expand to a Larger World   137
Widen Your Product Line   138
Be Different—and Win Big   139
People Are Your Hidden Resource   141

DAY 7

CHAPTER 7

OVERCOME ALL ROADBLOCKS TO YOUR FORTUNE MILLIONS   145

Lack of Money Can Be Overcome   146
How to Overcome Loan Turn-Downs   147
Where to Find Cosigners and Guarantors   149

Get Experienced People to Help You   151
Lack of Know-How Can Always Be Overcome   153
Get Good Legal and Accounting Advice   155
Direct Your Firm to Success   157
Good Advertising Brings Strong Results   158
Roadblocks Teach You How to Win   162

DAY 8

CHAPTER 8

BE A RESULTS PERSON EVERY DAY—AND MOVE AHEAD   167

Results Are the Key to Your Success   167
Set Up Daily Goals for Yourself   168
Control Results to Generate Millions   169
Get Your Business Plan Result   170
Find a Suitable Brokerage House   179
Sell Shares Yourself   181
Get Venture-Capital Results Quickly   182
Reach Free-Money Results Quickly   184
Get Breakout Financing Results   185
No-Credit-Check Lenders   186
Overseas Lenders Can Give You Money Results   189
Credit Unions Can Give You the Money Results You Seek   190
Use Asset-Based Lenders for Big-Money Results   191
Form an Offshore Bank to Attract Capital   193
Results *Are* the Name of Your Efforts   194

DAY 9

CHAPTER 9

BUILD ON YOUR EARLY SUCCESSES— AND ACQUIRE MORE WEALTH   199

Steady Progress Will Make You Rich   199
Popular Ways to Build on Early Success   201
Join the Takeover Boom   202
Three Ways to Get Rich from Takeovers   203

Use Company Money to Raise More Money   210
Become a Vacation Operator   215
Get Paid to Learn the Other Person's Business   218
Use Zero Cash to Build on Early Success   219

DAY 10

CHAPTER 10

SHARE YOUR SUCCESS
AND PROSPER RICHLY   225

Spread Your Wealth to Help Others—and Yourself   225
Hire People Other Firms Overlook   227
Sponsor Community Benefits   228
Buy Good Equipment for Your Business   229
Help Banks Get Rid of Repossessed Properties   230
Put Excess Funds into Programs Helping Others   232
Become a Member of Your Industry Associates   232
Lend Money to Other Businesses Needing It   234
Keep These Rules in Mind When You Lend   237
Become a Specialty Lender or Finder   238
Expand Your Services   240
Sharing Your Success Is a Great Payoff   242

BIBLIOGRAPHY   244

Other Profit-Building Tools   244
Newsletters   248
Success Kits   248
Order Form   255

INDEX   257

DAY 1

*H*ere—*on the first day of building* your *million-dollar fortune—you see that you get what you think. Your mind can make* you *rich—if you know what you want! Once you know that, you can easily decide how large an income you need. Knowing how much you want to earn, you can quickly pick the way to earn this income. And since most people don't have much capital, you're shown how to get* all *the money you need to earn the fortune you seek. Turn the page to start your million-dollar life in just 14 days—*now!

CHAPTER 1

TO BUILD GREAT WEALTH, KNOW WHAT YOU WANT

YOUR MIND CAN make you rich! Every week I see dozens of people who've built riches for themselves using the power of their mind. But each of these successful people knew—and knows—what he or she wants from life.

While you might be able to build riches without a plan, without knowing what you want, without a goal—the chances are very slim. So why not improve your chances by the thousands by knowing what you want!

You Get What You Think

Your mind can make you rich! I must repeat this for you often enough to make you believe the truth of this great statement.

You get what you think! Start thinking riches and you'll build riches. Think of driving your favorite luxury car and you'll soon find yourself behind the wheel of a shiny new model, tooling down the freeway!

My own successful life is a great example of getting what you think. Just let me give you a few examples of knowing what you want and getting what you think.

3

- At the age of 8 I decided I wanted to go to sea as a seaman in a merchant ship; at the age of 14 I shipped out on my first trip on the high seas.
- At the age of 21 I decided I should go to engineering school and get a degree. Six years later I graduated with honors in mechanical engineering.
- During a successful engineering career I decided to write a book on an important topic—pumps. Three years later the book was published. Today you'll find a dozen of my engineering books in every major public library in the world.
- Desiring to branch out from engineering, I decided to publish a newsletter for Beginning Wealth Builders (BWBs). Today this newsletter is nearly 25 years young. And it has brought me many millions in wealth while giving good jobs to a number of people.

I could go on. But I think you get the point. The secret is so simple that thousands of people spend years searching for it without ever learning that:

You can get anything you want in this life if you know what you want and then think of your goal every day while planning how to achieve your objective.

Since almost every major goal in life is based on money, my emphasis is on how you can get the money needed to reach your goal. And since most worthwhile goals require more money than you can earn from a job, I strongly suggest that you get your own business. Why? Well, think about it! With your own business:

- *You control your future* in terms of both money and time. Remember: You can never be too rich or too idle if you want to enjoy life!
- *You have greater freedom* because your only boss is your customer. Treat your customers well and they'll make you rich while giving you freedom to do what turns you on!
- *You have greater money freedom* since the business allows you to do as you please. You're not beholden to any petty, snarling, or carping boss!
- *You can't be fired, laid off, downsized,* or thrown out of work! And you need not fear losing the income that's so important to you and your family! Why? Because *you* control your income—not someone else!

Unless you know what you want, and think through to your ultimate goal, you really are wandering in the dark. As a reader recently told me:

> I was an officer in the Air Force with a dull urge to do more with my life. But I didn't know what I really wanted to do. Then, on your advice, I figured out what turned me on. It was model airplanes! So I decided to open a hobby shop at an Air Force base in Texas. The financing you provided got me started. Today I have two hobby shops and both are very successful. I'm doing what I want making money, and getting a lot of joy out of life. Thanks a million, Ty!

What Turns You On?

All of us have interests that turn us on. I've already told you about a few of mine. (There are plenty of others!)

But what about *you*? What's *your* "thing"? Is it music, boating, skiing, soccer, public speaking, fund raising, collecting Indian relics? The best way for you to figure out what turns you on is to use pencil and paper and:

1. *Take a ruled (lined) piece of paper* and list on it the following:
   a. What I like to do, best of all
   b. My second favorite activity
   c. My third favorite
2. *Transfer your favorite activity* to a new sheet of paper and list on it:
   a. Possible money-making aspects of your favorite
   b. Where you could make the money (home, store, etc.)
3. *Do the same* for your other two favorites.
4. *Put your papers aside* for a few days; during this time, think about what really turns you on: decide if there are other turn-ons that should have been listed instead of those you chose.
5. *If you find new interests* that are stronger than the first ones you listed, then put them to the same write-down and thinking tests you used for your first choices.

Now you're far ahead of when you started! Why? Because you know a lot more about yourself than you did earlier. But we want to be sure that your turn-ons will work. Let's get to that step next! Your turn-on sheets will look like those in Fig. 1-1 and 1-2.

Figure Out What You Really Want

You now know what turns you on—better than you ever knew before. But what do you really want from these turn-ons? Do you want to better your life through one or more of your turn-ons? If you do, you'll have lots of fun. And:

- *People who enjoy a hobby* and turn it into work earn more because they do a better job;
- *Which makes success breed success,* leading to greater overall satisfaction from life.

But do you really want to work at your hobby—your turn-on? Some people regard their turn-ons as almost sacred. When they're doing their thing, they're really living. Work cannot be allowed to interfere. So you must figure out what you really want. To find out what you really want, ask yourself these questions. Check off Yes or No as you answer them:

1. Do I really want to work at my turn-on?   _____ Yes   _____ No
2. Will working at my turn-on turn me off?   _____ Yes   _____ No
3. Does my turn-on know-how promise more business success?   _____ Yes   _____ No
4. Will I be satisfied making money from my turn-on?   _____ Yes   _____ No
5. Is there a large enough money-making potential in my turn-on business?   _____ Yes   _____ No

You should have at least three *Yes* answers to these questions. And if the answer to Question 5 is *No,* you should look for another turn-on that you might turn into a business. Why?

MY TURN-ON SHEET

1. My favorite activity is: *Watching adventure stories on TV*
2. My second favorite activity is: *Playing tennis and golf*
3. My third favorite activity is: *Jogging 80 miles per week*

Fig. 1-1   *Typical listing of favorite activities*

INCOME POSSIBILITIES OF
MY FAVORITE ACTIVITIES

Activity No. and Description	*Money-Making Possibilities*
1. Watching adventure stories on TV	a. Open video store specializing in adventure tapes
	b. Open general video store to rent all types of tapes
	c. Buy video rental store franchise to save time and money
2. Playing tennis and golf	a. Start tennis and/or golf pro shops in local area
	b. Give tennis or golf lessons to kids and/or adults
	c. Buy, or start, a tennis or golf club locally
3. Jogging 80 miles per week	a. Become a dealer for jogging supplies
	b. Develop or invent, and sell, in-home running equipment
	c. Organize jogging meets; charge entrance fee.

Fig. 1-2   *Business analysis of turn-ons. In actual work, each turn-on would have its own sheet for greater study.*

Because if the money-making potential is not there, you'll be wasting your time on a business that won't give you the life style you seek! As a reader recently wrote me:

> I always wanted the best in life. That's why I bought your book *How to Get Rich* and read it in an evening. Today I have a beautiful home, the best cars, and a ski business in Colorado. I love my business and I get a charge out of it every day. It gives me pleasure while allowing me to live in a way I enjoy. Thanks for all your guidance and help—and particularly for urging me to do "my thing" if it would pay me enough!

There's no sadder sight than seeing someone struggling at a business they love that doesn't pay them enough. Don't you get caught in the trap of working just for love! Even the best of love needs regular meals. So if you really want to make money from a turn-on, be sure the potential is there!

How Large an Income Do You Need?

Some people are satisfied with less income than others. In my years of building businesses and financing them for my readers I've noted that:

- *Income needs expand as you grow* happy with a life style you've picked for yourself.
- *Aiming at low income needs* almost always brings to you a small income.
- *Aiming at a high income* will almost always bring you a very high cash flow for as long as you want it.
- *Aiming higher costs no more.* And it could bring you the money and success you seek!

So figure out the income you need and then at least double it! Why? Because everything costs more as time goes by. Doubling your estimate will protect you against future cost increases.

Now what kinds of income estimates do I have in mind for you? I'm talking about income levels that:

- Start at $250,000 a year, and
- Go up to $1 million a year
- Depend on the type of business and the time you want to put into the business
- Because you really can't build great wealth starting at income levels below $250,000 per year.

To figure the income level you seek, take these easy steps right now, using the form below. Add the results to get the income you need.

1. Annual housing expense　　　　　　　　　$ _____
2. Annual food, clothing, entertainment　　$ _____
3. Other expected annual expenses　　　　　$ _____
4. Total annual expenses = 1 + 2 + 3 = x 5　$ _____
5. Now DOUBLE LINE 4 =　　　　　　　　　$ _____
   This is the annual income you should seek!

Remember: The annual income you need is *after*-income taxes. So you must figure how much income tax you'll have to pay on the income you seek. Then you'll have to earn that much more.

But the beauty of building great riches using the success action program we suggest to you in this book is that you can easily raise your income to the level you seek. So taxes aren't really a problem! What you're after is the money that stays in your hand!

So if an income level starting at $250,000 a year and going up from there interests you, let's take the next step in helping you acquire great wealth. You'll see how to use your mind to make yourself rich!

To show you what your annual income can do for your self-image and comfort, listen to this reader who writes:

> When I started with you I thought that $50,000 a year would put me in "heaven" since my income wasn't even one-tenth of that. But when I reached the $50,000 level you pushed me on to greater goals, saying "You can do it if you believe you can." Today I'm at $275,000 a year and still rising. I feel a new and great power in my life and my relationships. And my life style is a thousand times better than at the start. I'm really enjoying every part of my life since I have so much more freedom and fun. Thank you.

Five Steps to Your True Drives

Most BWBs (Beginning Wealth Builders) have only a vague idea of their true drives in life. You may know what you want—as we figured out earlier. But what drives you toward your goals? What pushes you toward great wealth? There must be a force.

If you understand your own drives you can more easily channel them into more productive money-making activities. Here's how to figure your drives and understand them better.

There are—as I see you—just five basic drives in BWBs. You probably have sensed these in yourself. These drives are:

1. *To make money*—usually large amounts in a short time in a business you like and enjoy
2. *To build security for yourself* by having an income that's dependable and can't be taken away
3. *To get the things you like*—that special auto, a dream home, boat, airplane, etc.
4. *To get ego satisfaction* from being the boss, "the top honcho," etc.
5. *To serve others* by delivering a needed product or useful service at a competitive price.

Do a bit of self-analysis by checking off below the degree of your drive in each of the listed areas. Then you'll have a much better idea of how—and where—to use the tips I give you on acquiring great wealth using your mind.

MY LIFE DRIVES

Drive I Have and Its Strength	Strong	Moderate	Weak
1. Making big money fast	_____	_____	_____
2. Build security for myself	_____	_____	_____
3. Get the things I want	_____	_____	_____
4. Ego satisfaction	_____	_____	_____
5. Serve others	_____	_____	_____

If you're like most BWBs I work with and help, you'll find that the first three drives—making money, building security, and getting things you want—are the strongest. If this is true of you, then you're reading the right book because

I'll show you—as I've shown thousands of others—exactly how to satisfy these drives while building great wealth!

Like this BWB, who writes a happy letter:

> I always wanted to own lots of real estate that would give me a big income. But with no starting capital it seemed impossible. Yet today—thanks to your help—I own over $6 million in real estate, which gives me an income of $100,000 a year. And I'm still building my real estate holdings because I want a larger income—soon!

Go Where Your Interests Push You

You know what you want in life, you've figured how large an income you'd like to have, and you know your true drives. If you were to call me up—as so many of my readers do, using my 800 number—I'm sure you'd tell me:

- I want to make a lot of money—soon.
- I'm doing what I enjoy.
- And right now I'm interested in real estate, or mail order, or import-export, or some other business.

Do you know what my answer to you would be? Without a moment's hesitation? It would be:

> **Go and do what your interests push you into doing. You'll be much more successful and you'll have a lot more fun!**

Following their interests, thousands of my BWB friends have built great wealth in:

- Real estate
- Mail order
- Import-export
- Financial brokerage
- Consulting
- Etc.

I want *you* to do the same—doing what interests you. Since you have a good idea of what turns you on, our next step is to get you started acquiring great wealth using the power of your mind. Then perhaps you can write me a letter like this one:

> I just finished my first export deal. I sold a new hospital $800,000 worth of basic supplies. Things like small bandages, needles, tubing, etc. I'll never see one item I'm exporting since the supplier is doing all the shipping. But I'll certainly see the 10%, or $80,000, commission I'm earning. And I want to thank you for the book *Worldwide Riches Opportunities* because I got the lead for this sale from that book.

This reader, who was in the jewelry business before he started exporting, made a decision to branch out into a field that interested him. Exporting was that field. Going where his interests pushed him helped him earn a nice fee for his first sale! You—I'm convinced—can do much the same. And I'm here to help you along the way, just as I helped the above BWB.

Pick the Best Way to Build Your Wealth

Many BWBs think that the best way to build wealth is to get a "secure" job and work hard. No, friend, it just doesn't work that way! Why? Because:

- *"Secure jobs"* are rare these days—even in civil service; there are too many staff cuts and other reductions in personnel for any job to be secure.
- *No job ever rewards you* to the extent you deserve. Result? You never earn as much as you should.
- *Being a wage slave* on a job rarely makes a person rich. The employer takes too much of the profit for you to be paid at a level that will make you wealthy.

So save time—here and now—and give up any hope of making big money on the job. The only road to big money is your own business!

Now don't let the idea of having your own business scare you! Why? Because, as you'll realize when you think about it, having your own business:

- *Gives you great freedom* over your time and over your movements
- *Allows you to take home* most of the profits you earn by working smarter

- ***Helps you get away*** from stupid, complaining, and unappreciative bosses
- ***Puts you in line*** to earn a large fortune if your business ideas catch on with your customers.

So stop fearing your own business. Having a business can give you the greatest charge of joy you've ever had in your life! And if you pick your business carefully—using the guidelines and help I give you—there's little chance that you'll run into serious trouble.

Now that I've convinced you that having your own business is "the way to make it today," let's put *you* into the right business! It's easier than you think. As one reader writes:

> Once I found the right business for me, I started earning more in one week than I earned in a month on a job. But what's more, I really enjoy my business. I look forward to going to work every day. I no longer have to drag my body into a place I hate!

How to Get Your Own Business

You know—based on your reading of the first few pages of this book—the following:

- If you want to work at your "turn-on"
- The annual income you need to live as you wish
- What your major drives are.

With this information in hand you should be able to pick a business that interests you. Of course, if you've always wanted to make money in real estate (we'll say), or some other favorite business, your choice is already made for you.

Your next question is:

- Should I start my own business?
- Or should I buy a going business?

There's no perfect answer to this question. But my experience with thousands of BWBs shows:

Buying a going business is usually a little safer for most

BWBs because it's easier to predict future results from past performance than it is to project from the unknown.

If you go along with my experience—and that of thousands of BWBs around the world, then you're immediately faced with a task. What's that task? Simply, it's:

Raising the money for the down payment on the going business is the first bit of work you'll have after choosing the type of business you want to use to make your fortune.

Since I've helped thousands of BWBs get the money they needed for a business or real-estate deal, I'm ready to help you, too! And this help won't cost you anything. As one of my BWB readers recently told me on the phone:

I got a $4-million loan with just 3 telephone calls using the info you gave me. Thanks a million!

Did this reader have to pay me a fee for finding him this $4-million loan? The answer is *NO!* I never accept fees for getting loans for people. My business is publishing. I make my money by selling information. Yet I've helped many people get big loans without ever asking (or accepting) a penny in fees.

If you want to know what business this reader is in, I'll tell you. It's import-export and his firm is a startup—that is, he hasn't made a cent in sales yet. But he did get his loan on the basis of the tip I gave him! You—I'm convinced—can do the same. Just follow my pointers and you'll get what you seek in life!

Understand Financing and Get Money

You started this book by getting a better understanding of yourself. With that in your control, you can then turn to money—the key to all business success. As understanding yourself is so important for your success, so too is understanding financing. Let's get you the understanding so you get the money you seek!

Money for business comes in two general ways to you.

Understanding the differences can put big bucks into your pocket. The two forms of business money are:

- *Loans*—Where money is "rented" to you for a given time for a specific purpose. You repay the money to your lender on either a monthly or annual basis. Your "rent" is the interest the lender charges on the loan. Every loan *must* be repaid in full.
- *Equity money* is cash put into your business in the form of ownership. The investor buys part of your business with the hope that it will grow and the portion will be worth more than was paid for it. Equity money *never* need be repaid. Instead, the investor looks to the growth of the business as the source of the repayment. Most equity investments are made in corporations. But some partnerships also attract equity investments.

As a BWB—Beginning Wealth Builder, in case you forgot— a loan is a little easier to get than equity money. Why? Because:

- *Loans* are the recognized source of funding for most small or new businesses. So when you apply for a loan, people understand your situation. You don't have to do a lot of explaining.
- *Equity money* is available for small and new businesses. But you must have a business plan and a very promising idea for your business to get equity money quickly and easily. Yet plenty of new small companies *do* get equity money when they seek it in the right way—which we tell you about later in this book.

To get a loan you need to take over a going business, or start a new business, there are certain easy steps for you to take. These easy steps are:

1. *Figure out* how much money you need. If you don't know how much to ask for, you're almost certain *not* to get your loan!
2. *Have a specific purpose* for your loan. And make sure this purpose is one that lenders know and are comfortable with in their lending. In a few moments I'll give you acceptable loan purposes.
3. *Pick suitable lenders.* The lenders you ask to make your loan should be making the type of loan you seek. While

this may seem simple, you'd be amazed at how many BWBs come to me and say: "I tried 10 lenders and all said no. Why?" When I ask about the lenders they tried, I quickly find they asked *business* lenders for a *real-estate* mortgage! It doesn't work that way. You go to a real-estate lender for a real-estate loan—*not* a business lender!

4. *Type your loan application*—or get someone to type it for you. Sitting on the lender's side of the desk, I can tell you that a typed app (as we call them) gets faster attention and much more reading than a scrawled handwritten app that one has to squint at to read!

5. *Be completely truthful* on your application. If you aren't, the lender may turn off—forever. Why risk such a rejection when all you need do is tell the truth?

Loan Helps You Can Use

To help you get the loan you seek, I'm available to you—day or night—if you're a subscriber to my monthly newsletter, *International Wealth Success*. Costing only $24 a year for 12 issues, it gives *you* dozens of active lenders in every issue. As a subscriber, you can get a free evaluation of any loan application you are considering. I do this evaluation myself and either call you or send you (whichever *you* prefer) my views on how the app might be improved. To subscribe to the newsletter, send $24 to IWS, Inc., POB 186, Merrick, NY 11566. You'll get your first issue quickly.

Other loan helps you can use include these:

1. *Check your local bank*—ask what types of business or real-estate loans they make. Also ask them to send you a sample loan application for the type of loan you seek—if they make such loans. You can do this checking either by phone or mail. Of course, if you want to visit the bank in person, you can also do that. But it takes longer because you often have to stand around waiting for a loan officer.

2. *Get free info from business development companies.* Every state today has a business development plan through which they encourage new businesses. Many such plans include low-interest-rate loans for startup and

existing businesses in the state. You will often be able to "float" a loan through a business development company much more easily than through a bank. To get the names and addresses of such companies, order a copy of *Business Capital Sources,* described at the back of this book.

3. *Contact local mortgage lenders*—if real estate is your turn on. *Remember: Everybody* finances real estate! Why shouldn't you? Real-estate money is probably the easiest kind to get today because—as we just said—everybody finances real estate! If you have trouble locating local real-estate lenders, get a copy of *2,500 Active Real Estate Lenders,* described at the back of this book. It may just get you the loan you need for your real-estate fortune!

4. *See if the Small Business Administration* will make, or guarantee, the loan you need. And, good friend, SBA *does* make loans for factory buildings and other production facilities, besides—of course—for machinery, vehicles, and a variety of other purposes. Further, SBA has speeded its approval procedures. This means that you can often get your loan or guarantee quickly.

5. *Apply at a local SBIC*—Small Business Investment Company—for help. These firms are chartered by the SBA but have capital of their own (in most cases) that they lend out to local and national firms. Your firm— hopefully—might be one of those they'll lend to when you apply—using a typed application! To get the names, addresses, telephone numbers, and lending guides for over 400 SBICs, get a copy of *SBIC Directory and Small Business Handbook* listed at the back of this book.

Do these loan helps work? They sure do! Many of my readers report to me that they:

- *Got an SBA loan,* or guarantee, using the ideas given above
- *Obtained a bank loan* for a business in a matter of hours— with almost *no* trouble of any kind
- *Financed excellent real estate* using a mortgage loan from one of the sources we gave them
- *Raised venture capital* in the form of a loan that did not have to be repaid if the business made money.

Truly, good friend (*all* my readers are friends since we think alike), the money for your fortune building *is* available to *you!* And I'm ready to help you get it. Just test me, as a reader did who called to say:

> I'm just calling you to see if you really exist. (I do!) I want to know if you're really there. So you can look forward to more calls when I have some questions for you!

Loan helps you can use are as close as your telephone or mailbox. Just remember:

- *You must know what you want.* All the loan helps in the world are useless unless you know what you want.
- *Pick the way you want to build wealth* before you rush out to raise money; if you don't know what you want to do, lenders won't want to work with you.

Then perhaps you can write me letters like these:

> Ty, since I've been taking the *International Wealth Success* newsletter I bought two 5-plexes and realize a positive cash flow of over $750 a month on a low investment. Not bad for plastic money. Since then I've been offered three-quarters of a city block with 20 rentals on it.

And,

> Almost a year ago, I borrowed $40,000 in about three minutes, when I was 22 years old.

And,

> Things are working out just as you said. "No cash down" *is* possible. I bought 25 acres of prime land without one cent of mine.

And,

> Following your plan, I've amazed myself, Ty. As I said on the phone, I placed an $8 ad in the local paper and sold over $4,000 in products. Without the guidelines in your books, who knows what would have happened?

And,

> My ad in the *IWS* newsletter sold over 8,000 lamps at $7 each. Your newsletter sure brings *results!*

And,

I got the $350,000 loan I told you about because I used
your methods and your *Business Plan Kit*. The lender told
me it was the best business plan he ever saw and he simply
could not refuse to make the loan! Thanks so much!

Have an Acceptable Purpose for Your Loan

Banks and other lenders do *not* lend money for trivial
purposes. So you can't borrow money to bet at the race track,
take a flyer in the stock market, etc. But banks and other
lenders *do* lend money for these very acceptable purposes:

- *Purchase* of machinery, vehicles, office equipment
- *Expansion* of your business through more people, stronger
  marketing efforts, staff training
- *Long-term mortgages*—15-, 20-, 25-, 30-, and 40-years for
  factories, offices, stores, etc.
- *Personal use*—such as vacation, home improvement,
  medical, dental, education, debt consolidation, etc.
- *Home equity* takeouts where you get either a line of credit
  or a direct loan for any sensible purposes you may have
  in mind.

If you think about these purposes, you'll see that they're
all helpful to a business or real-estate deal. That's what lenders
are happy to make loans for—beneficial purposes. So be sure
that your loan purpose *is* useful. Then you'll have a much
greater chance of getting the loan you seek.

Keep in mind at *all* times that Ty Hicks—me—is here,
ready and able to help *you* get the loan you seek. As a reader
of my books and newsletter you have a special place in my
world. So I want to help *you* in every way I can!

Let me leave you with one last thought about getting loans.
That thought is this:

> *If you can't get a loan on your own, try a financial broker
> or financial consultant. Such a person or firm might be able
> to help you. Or you might even try becoming a financial
> broker yourself to raise money for your deals!*

Thus, a young ambitious reader who bought our *Financial
Broker, Finder, Business Broker, Business Consultant Kit* (see

the back of this book) writes, a few weeks after receiving the Kit:

> To this date, I have made nearly a million and a quarter dollars in loans (all by phone), and things are getting better every day.

Raise Nonrepayable Capital

As you'll recall, we said earlier that the second type of capital for your business is nonrepayable. It's called equity capital. With such money, people buy into your business. And as part owners they share in the profits your business earns.

But don't worry. You do *not* lose control of your business when you get equity capital! Why? Because:

- You can sell less than a controlling interest—under 50% of the stock.
- Few outside buyers want to run your business on a day-to-day basis—they just want their investment to grow as large and as fast as possible.
- Many people quickly forget the investment they made in your business. So they don't "bug" you on a regular basis—they leave you free to run your business!

Now how can you get equity capital? There are three ways. And only the first is true equity capital. The second two ways produce the same effect as equity capital but—strictly speaking—they are not included under the usual type of equity capital. Yet their importance to you is the same. That's why I'm suggesting you consider them. The three ways to get equity capital are:

1. **Sell stock** in your corporation to either public or private investors.
2. **Sell limited partnership shares** to public or private investors.
3. **Get business grants** for your firm based on the work you do for the benefit of some segment of the population.

Now, when we say "sell" stock or shares in your firm,

we're *not* suggesting that you do the selling! You can—if
you wish. But—usually—the selling is done by an experienced
salesperson who has customers already lined up. So don't
be frightened by the idea of having to sell.

But—as an aside—I might say that some of the best business
experience I ever obtained was as a boy selling housewares
door-to-door. There's no better experience—in my view—than
having to charge yourself up to go to the next house after
having five doors in a row slammed in your face! Remember:
Your mind can make you rich. In door-to-door selling you
really need mind control if you are to succeed.

Now let's take a quick look at each type of equity capital
and the amount of money it might deliver to *your* business
for your use. You may want to use one, or all, methods.

Sell Stock in Your Corporation

Your firm *must* be a full corporation to raise money by
selling stock to public or private investors. And you *must*
have the help of a competent attorney to organize a
corporation. Forget about doing it yourself! It's too dangerous.

Once your corporation is being formed, you can decide
how many shares of stock to issue. Most states will allow
you to issue as many shares as you choose. So you can issue
anywhere from 100 shares to 50 million shares, if you wish.
The number is included in the corporate charter. If you decide
to issue a small number of shares at the start, you can always
go back and revise your charter to include a larger number
of shares later. Remember:

> *Since your company is probably a startup, you will either*
> *sell a large number of shares at a low price per share to*
> *the public, or a small number of shares at a high price per*
> *share in a private offering. So you should have a good idea*
> *of how your shares will be sold* before you finalize your
> corporate charter.

Now let's get a few common misbeliefs out of the way.
To make a successful public offering and raise as much as
$5 million the first year:

- *Your firm does not have* to have a sales history. Plenty of firms go public with no sales—only debts!
- *No fancy offices,* factories, or other facilities are needed to go public. Sometimes the poorer your firm, the easier it is to raise money from the public!
- *Public offerings take time*—typically 90 days to raise $5 million. Private offerings go much faster. You can raise $50 million (ten times the $5 million) in just 48 hours with a private offering. The key to success? A highly saleable product, service, or idea.

What steps should you take if you want to go public or raise money via a private offering? Here are the simple steps for you:

1. *Prepare a simple business plan* telling what business you'll go into, how much money you'll need, what level of profits you expect. Use the *Business Plan Kit* listed at the back of this book as a guide.
2. *Contact a competent attorney* who knows corporate law and formation rules for your area. Tell the attorney what you want to do with regard to raising money.
3. *Decide, with your attorney's help,* how you'll get the money—by a public or private offering.
4. *Send your business plan* to a brokerage house that might handle your offer. You'll find such houses listed in the *Wall Street Syndicators* booklet listed at the back of this book. Or you can look in your local "Yellow Pages" under "Stock Brokers" for the phone numbers of brokerage houses that might help you. Call or write each, telling what you want to do.
5. *Work out a deal* and get your money. The brokerage house should be able to recommend the best deal for your firm—public or private offering. Follow the advice you get, after consulting with your attorney. Just be sure that *all* costs, including your attorney's fee, come out of the proceeds of your offering! That way the deal won't cost you a dime. I'm a great believer in 100% financing of all business transactions.

Now that you know how to go public, let me say one more thing. Don't listen to people who tell you: "It can't be done. You can't take a new firm public." Most of these people don't know what they're talking about. They just let their mouths flap in the wind! And to help you better cope with such critics, we give you a lot more info on going public in Chapter 8 of this book.

Plenty of my readers *have* gone public and *have* raised money for a new firm that had *no* sales of any kind! And these readers have done much of the work themselves, with the guidance of a competent attorney. I speak from real, firing-line experience. Ask your critics if they've ever had any real experience in this business!

Use Limited Partners to Get Money

A limited partnership is easier to form than a corporation. But—again—you *must* have the advice and counsel of a competent attorney. You can form a limited partnership yourself with just a few pieces of paper, available at most business stationery supply houses. But you're playing with a nuclear device that can go off at any moment if you don't have a qualified attorney. In a limited partnership:

- *Partners put money into the firm* in amounts that usually range from $5,000 per partner to as much as $5 million per partner. Usual ranges—however—are $5,000 to $50,000 per partner.
- *You would be the General Partner* in such a firm. As such, you're responsible for the day-to-day operation of the business and the partnership. Your limited partners won't bother you much since all they want is to see their investment grow in value.
- *You can put your investment* into the partnership in the form of your ideas, work, and energy—all of which have value. And you can share in the profits, just as other partners do!
- *Shares in the partnership* can be sold to the public, or to private parties. Almost all limited partnership shares are sold privately since the deal is much faster and much simpler.

Get Hard-Cash Grants

If your business will help others in areas such as health, housing, historic preservation, etc., you may be able to get a hard-cash grant. A grant gives you money that:

- *Need never be repaid* if you do the work for which the grant was made
- *Can cover all your costs* for doing the work—such as labor, materials, supplies, rent, heat, etc.
- *Will be renewed* with little effort if the work is to be continued over a period of time.

You can apply for grants at a number of sources. Usual sources that make grants year after year include the:

- Federal government
- State governments
- Large corporations in the United States
- Foundations set up to make grants.

Some of my readers have obtained grants in amounts of hundreds of thousands of dollars for less than two pages of typed facts! Others have obtained grants in lower amounts for similar short, concise proposals. You may be able to do the same—if your firm will do work that helps others.

One of the fastest ways to get grants today is to use what I call my "Phone-In/Mail-In" technique. Here's what you do:

1. *Decide* how large a grant you need; if you don't know how much money you need, you won't have much luck getting it.
2. *Pick* the source(s) for your grant. You should start with the typical sources listed above.
3. *Write,* or have someone else write, a short proposal telling what you propose to do, why the work is needed, who will benefit, and what the cost will be for the work. Keep the proposal to no more than two typed pages.
4. *Call,* or write, your selected grant sources. Ask if they'd be interested in the type of grant you have in mind. If the answer is yes, send your proposal to the grantor; wait for an answer!

Grants are very useful to any business. You can increase your chances of getting a suitable grant by using the *Phone-In/Mail-In Grants Kit* listed at the back of this book. It gives you many examples of winning proposals that you might use to get your grant. *And remember: Grant money never need be repaid, if you do the work for which the grant was made.*

Move Ahead to Your Wealth

You now know a lot more about yourself and your money drives. You're ready to move to the next step of your success action program to build a million-dollar fortune. Knowing that your mind can make you rich, you just have to put it to work earning your riches—in 14 days, or less!

Remember at all times: You have a friend in your author. If you run into any problems, I'm always here to help you. And I *do* always want to help every BWB (Beginning Wealth Builder) who's sincere about building riches quickly in his or her own business. Now let's make your mind plans real!

(But let me add just one point: I can help you finance your business or make you a grant for your business, if you read my newsletter. Details on these two plans are given later in this book.)

DAY 2

You need a plan for every business you start or take over. Once you have a good plan, you can almost coast to your million-dollar fortune. So on your second day of your 14-day success action program you'll see how to prepare a winning plan for your business. You can do this quickly—or you can have someone do it for you. The main idea though is this: Your mind can make you rich if you have a good business plan that charts the way to your great riches!

CHAPTER 2

PLAN YOUR SUCCESS— AND WORK YOUR PLAN

SOME PEOPLE TRY to stumble through life, hoping that Lady Luck will guide them to a big gold mine. It seldom happens! A person without a plan for his or her success just drifts on an endless sea. You probably know plenty of people like this.

A person with a plan for his or her life—especially in the money area—moves ahead much faster, and far more surely. Lady Luck seems to find these people and help them almost every day! You should have a plan for your business success since it can almost guarantee that you'll hit the big money. Let's see why a business plan can be so important to your fortune building.

You Always Need a Plan

If you want to drive from a known city to an unknown one, you need a plan of some kind to get there. A simple road map *is* a plan, if followed for a specific route. Thus, you might take the quickest or most direct route. Or you might take the scenic route, which gives you breathtaking views of the mountains and valleys, or the sea. With either choice, you *do* know how to get from your known city to the unknown one (Point A to Point B) because you have a plan—your road map.

Likewise in your business life, when you're building a fortune, a business plan will:

- **Show** you which steps to take to build your fortune in your chosen business
- **Predict** your future income and expenses so you'll know what you'll need to keep your business going
- **Guide** you in taking action that will increase your income so you take more money home every day of the year.

Some BWBs (Beginning Wealth Builders) resist business plans, saying: "I'll get around to that when my income is big enough. Meanwhile, all I want to do is make money!"

Making money is all any of us want to do, including your author! But, good friend, it's a lot easier and a lot faster if you have a plan! And this plan can be just a few lines jotted on a scrap of paper. It doesn't need to be a fat book! Once you do your plan you may tell me, as one reader did:

> I hated you the day you told me that I should have a business plan. It was like being told to go back to school. But when I saw your yacht I said to myself "If this guy can drive a yacht that big he may know what he's talking about." So I roughed out a quick plan in pencil. Not only was it fun to do but I saw things about my business I'd never thought of. Thanks; my business is booming—like never before!

Good Business Plans Can Make You Millions

If you want to get a loan, if you want to raise money from the public that never need be repaid, if you want to get a grant that never need be paid back, you need a business plan! Good friend, there's no way you can avoid this basic need. Planning is a *must* if you want to be successful.

Plenty of my readers report—again and again—successes that follow this general line:

> I showed them my business plan and within 24 hours I had $3 million in funding for my idea. No sweat—they just gave my company the money, after I signed some papers covering membership on the Board of Directors and voting

rights. The business plan was what got the money for me and my company. Thanks for pushing me to do it!

Now a good business plan need not be hundreds of pages in length. You can raise millions with just a 10-page plan. If you need more space, then let your business plan go to 20 pages. But don't go beyond 25 pages unless you're looking for bigger money—$50 million or more!

When you plan your life and your business, you show other people that you're in control. Why? Because:

- *Planning* is work—you must think about what you'll do in the future, based on what you know now.
- *Everyone* who controls money knows that planning is work. So they have great respect for someone who plans well.
- *Getting money* is much easier when the people who control that money respect you.

So even if you're trying to raise smaller amounts of money—in the hundreds or thousands of dollars, planning pays off. With a plan you know:

- *Where* you're going
- *How* you'll get there
- *When* you'll arrive
- *What* amount of money you'll have
- *Which* competitors will give you problems
- *Where* your money will be coming from
- *Why* you're working to achieve your goal.

Another reader says, about her business plan:

My business plan opened doors for me that would never have even been unlocked without it. Just the fact that I could say "Should I send you a copy of my business plan?" made people sit up and take notice. Two venture capitalists almost threw $600,000 into my face within hours after they saw my plan. It really worked for me!

What Your Business Plan Should Cover

Writing a business plan—whether you do it yourself or have someone else write it for you—is easy. Why? Because:

- Most business plans follow a standard outline.
- All that need be done is fill in data on your business, using the standard outline.
- Following the standard outline makes you come up with the needed information to get the money you seek for your business.

While the outline you'll see for business plans may differ slightly from one source to another, the "standard" outline is:

1. Executive Summary
2. Description of the Business
3. Competitors in the Business
4. Management Available
5. Funding Needed
6. Use of Funds Raised
7. Income and Expense Projections
8. Financial Summaries.

Now don't let this outline frighten you! If you've done any thinking about your business, it will be easy to fill in most of the blanks. And you can use the *Business Planner Kit,* described at the end of this book, as an excellent guide to either preparing the plan yourself or having someone else do it for you. Every BWB (Beginning Wealth Builder) I've worked with (and there are many, many thousands all over the world) beamed with joy once he or she finished a business plan.

Why? Because they now had their business future within their own control. Having a finished plan in hand makes you feel ready to meet any challenge. Nothing—not even raising money—frightens you! Somehow you know you'll get every penny of the money you need.

Now that you know what your business plan should contain, let's see how to start your plan. *Remember this:* Your mind can make you rich! Thinking through your business plan, using your mind, *can* make *you* rich!

How to Start Your Business Plan

The most powerful part of any business plan is the Executive Summary. This is the part in which you use 500, or fewer, words to tell what your future business will do, how much money is needed, and what results an investor can expect. Many times you'll get your money just on the basis of the Executive Summary—nothing else! So it's a very good place to start.

Now don't let the words "Executive Summary" put you off. I'll be glad to write—free of charge—your Executive Summary if you're a subscriber to my monthly newsletter, *International Wealth Success,* described later. All I need from you is info about your business and I'll prepare your Executive summary in a day, or less. Since I must spend time and energy writing your Executive Summary, I ask that you be a two-year subscriber to the newsletter.

Why is your Executive Summary so important? For a number of reasons, namely:

- Many money investment decisions to put funds into your company are made after reading your Executive Summary.
- If your Executive Summary is good, people will often say "This is it! Let's put money into this business right now."
- People are so rushed these days they will seldom have time to read much more than your Executive Summary before making a decision.

Using the Executive Summary, I've seen BWBs in all parts of the world raise big chunks of money, like these:

- $11.7 million was raised by a leading-edge technology company to fund a startup.
- A small vending company raised $250,000 in a private offering in which the Executive Summary was an important element of the decision.
- A publisher raised $3 million from some of his customers to start a financial services company, using his Executive Summary as a sales tool.

Now what will you say in your Executive Summary? You'll say much of what is said in this recent summary I wrote for an *IWS* subscriber:

Executive Summary

Fireside Services is a startup company that provides fireplace tools, decorations, safety equipment, and design services for home owners in the northern sections of the country. With the greater emphasis on home entertaining, Fireside Services sees a market of $6 million a year for its products two years after opening. To balance the seasonal nature of its winter business, Fireside will offer air conditioning maintenance and service facilities during warm weather.

Fireside Services seeks $1.5-million startup capital to buy equipment (3 trucks, office furniture, computer, and related items), establish a working capital fund, and pay for initial advertising. Projections show that this money could easily be repaid within three years after opening of the business.

A strong management team with much experience in fireplace and air conditioning design, installation, and operation is available. This management team is ready to start as soon as funding is completed.

Long-range financial projections show gross sales of $10 million in the fifth year of the company's life. Profits are expected to be strong since the overhead in the business is extremely low. The reason for this is that most of the work is done on the customer's premises, where the rent and power costs are zero.

A full business plan is available for this opportunity from John Gray, 123 Main St., Anytown 00000; tel 200-234-5678. All inquiries are welcome and will be answered.

There you have an Executive Summary of only 233 words, yet it tells a full story. Let's see how you can come up with an equally good Executive Summary for your money-making business that will free you from a life of cranky bosses.

Doing Your Executive Summary

Let's start with a promise from your author. My promise to you, as my reader, is this:

If you have a good business idea for either starting or buying a profitable activity, I will be glad to write your Executive

Summary to help you get loan or equity money if you're a subscriber to my newsletter or the buyer of one of my kits. There is no charge of any kind for this service.

But I do think you should do your own Executive Summary—if you can. Why? Because you'll learn a lot by doing it. To do your own Summary, take these easy steps:

1. *Gather data* on your business from every source you can—such as from other owners of similar businesses; the seller, if one is involved; reference books on the business you like; etc.
2. *Make estimates* of the sales you'll reach in 1 year, 2 years, 3 years, and 5 years. Do this by figuring how many customers and sales you'll have each week of the year, allowing for expected slow times.
3. *Figure the costs* you'll have in the business for labor, rent, supplies, advertising, etc., for each month of the year. Be accurate in your figuring.
4. *Compute your profit* using the figures in steps 2 and 3, above. Your business *must* show a profit estimate of at least 15% before taxes. Why? Because at any lower profit percentage, lenders won't be too interested in working with you. And equity capital providers will have about the same view!
5. *Get information* on your management team. The people who'll be working with you should have a strong background in the business. Without people with previous experience, it will be hard to convince lenders that you have the winning combination!
6. *Take a pass* at writing your Executive Summary. This is really easy if you follow my five-paragrah outline, given below.

Five Paragraphs to Potential Millions

You *can* do a selling Executive Summary in less than 250 words. Just use this painless outline:

Paragraph 1: Tell what the company does, why its sales will be strong, what sales level will be reached in the first two years, and any other positive features of the company's future.

See the first paragraph of the Fireside Services Summary, earlier in this chapter.

Paragraph 2: Tell how much money is needed, for what uses, and how quickly the money could be repaid, if the funding is a loan. Again, see the Fireside Services Summary for a good example.

Paragraph 3: Give info on your management team. Your people *should* have experience in the field!

Paragraph 4: Tell what sales you project for the fifth year of business. Why? Because lenders and venture capitalists think in terms of one year and five years. Also give an estimate of your profits for the fifth year—again, for the same reason. And give any other positive features that will make profits better.

Paragraph 5: The easy one! Just tell your reader where he or she can get more data on your company.

With just these five paragraphs you might be able to raise millions! "Can't be so," you say? Well listen to me, good friend. I've seen an Executive Summary raise millions in these businesses for BWBs:

- **Real estate** of all types—residential (apartment houses), commercial (stores and shopping centers), industrial (factories, docks, and industrial parks)
- **Mail order** of all types—publishing, sale of medicines, toys, marine products for boaters, newsletters, etc.
- **Import-export**—selling products and services all over the world for high profits. The items sold *helped* people— that is, they were *not* guns, tanks, or fighter planes!
- **Electronics products** of many types—both consumer (TV, VCR, radios, etc.) and industrial (security cameras, test equipment, etc.). Big fortunes have been made selling personal computers to both consumers and business customers, starting with capital raised by a clear, concise Executive Summary.
- **Services of many types,** both personal and business, can raise money via the Executive Summary. Just follow the outline above for best results!

Of course, the Executive Summary will be followed up by a complete business plan. But the Executive Summary is the foot-in-the-door that can get you the money you need. As this BWB lady told me:

> My costume jewelry business needed money in the worst way. But the more I talked to lenders, the clearer it became to me that they all wanted something in writing beyond the usual loan application. That's when I spoke to you and you promised to write my Executive Summary if I supplied you info on my business. And lo and behold, the first lender who saw my summary made the loan I asked for! In fact, he even offered me more, if I needed it. But I declined, not wanting to take on a bigger payment burden than I could handle.

At my company, International Wealth Success, Inc., we have funded by loans a number of businesses. And each of these sent me a neat, concise Executive Summary. Our loans are currently made at 12% simple interest for up to 7 years. The amount can go to $500,000. And interest-only payments are acceptable, with a balloon payment in the last month.

Every loan we've ever made (for more than 22 years at this writing) has been repaid by the happy borrower. All we ask is that the loan be for *active* business or real-estate purposes. By that we mean that the money be used to:

- Start a new business
- Buy a going business
- Buy income real estate of some kind
- Expand a business or rehab a real-estate project
- Increase the number of jobs a business provides
- Raise sales of a business by advertising or promotion
- Be used for any other productive business or real-estate purpose where money is earned.

Where a business is in trouble, we also make business emergency loans. These loans are at 6% simple interest for the same 7 years, up to $500,000. And interest-only repayment can be made, if you want. With these loans, there must be some hope that the money will help the business improve.

Other features of these loans for active business and real-estate purposes are:

- *No points;* no fees; no front money of any kind is every charged; nor are there ever any requests for "loan processing fees," "loan application fees," etc.
- *The loan is made by certified check* sent to the borrower by registered mail.
- *Time required* to make a loan can be as short as four (4) hours after receipt of the loan application and any other documents needed. The usual time for loan approval is one day. If desired, the money can be wired into the borrower's bank account. To do this, the lender must be supplied with the name of the bank, name of the account, and number of the account.

To apply for these business or real-estate loans, we ask that the borrower be a two-year, or longer, subscriber to our newsletter, *International Wealth Success.* So send $48 for a two-year subscription (24 issues) to IWS, Inc., POB 186, Merrick NY 11566-0186. Ask for our loan application and it will be sent to you immediately. The monthly newsletter will keep you informed on developments in business and planning so you're right up to date! (You'll find more info on our loans later in this book.)

So you better understand the meaning of *active* business or real-estate purposes for these loans, here are a number of examples of purposes for actual loans we've made:

- Buy printing equipment to expand a printing firm
- Buy an X-ray machine for a medical practice
- Open a hobby shop in a densely populated area
- Expand a successful architectural practice
- Put a down payment on income real estate
- Start an import-export company
- Buy, and operate, a commercial fishing boat
- Open a fast-food restaurant

There are—of course—many other purposes for which loans were, and are, made. But the above reasons give you a typical cross section of purposes.

Other, free services that two-year subscribers to the newsletter get in addition to those mentioned above, include:

- *Loan-by-phone telephone approval* of loan applications after the application is filled out. In other words, all you

need do is call me and read off the data on your loan application and I can tell you *yes*, we can make your loan; or *no*, you need this or that before I can say yes.
- **Six-month free review** of your loan application, if—for some reason—it was declined
- **Full loan data info** on how, and why, these loans are made for active business and real-estate use
- **Overnight delivery of your loan check**, if you want fast service—at *no* charge of any kind to you

Now let's turn to finishing your business plan. As you know, your mind *can* make you rich. And planning really *does* work!

Doing the Rest of Your Plan

You already know the other main sections of your plan. Let's look at each quickly and see what's in it. While we'd like to include a complete actual business plan, we don't have room for it. You'll find actual plans in the *Business Planner Kit*, mentioned earlier.

The second section on your business plan is a description of the business. In this section, tell in simple terms:

- **What the business is,** who it serves, what its growth trends are, typical sales levels achieved, and why you want to go into the business. Describe the business as though your reader knows nothing about it.
- **Take nothing for granted** in your description. Make the business crystal clear to anyone who's thinking of making you a loan or investing equity (venture) capital in it.

Next, tell who else is in the business. That is, name your competitors. And remember this:

- **The more competitors you have,** the better your chances of getting the money! Why? Because the more people there are in a business, the larger the market. With a large market, there's a greater chance to hit the big bucks.
- **In some new, leading-edge businesses,** there may be no competitors yet. If that's the case for you, tell your readers this, saying: "This business is so new there are no

competitors yet. But we do expect a number to come into the field as soon as its potential is realized."

From the competition, you move into your management team. If you're a loner, this may give you problems. But they're easy to handle—thus:

- "The company," you write, "is new and is managed by the founder, _____(Your Name)_____ . As soon as growth is sufficient, qualified management personnel will be hired to conduct the company's business profitably."

If you already have a management team in mind, you write differently. You say:

- "A highly competent management team is ready to move into action. This team consists of:" Here you name each person in the team and give a brief resume of his or her business qualifications and skills. Don't be afraid to list everyone's educational and business accomplishments. Lenders and investors love this kind of information.

Now you move into the funding needed. When doing this section, be very careful to remember:

- *You can't raise money* unless you know how much you need! While this may seem like a simple concept, many BWBs overlook this important fact.
- *Ask for more than you need.* Money needs have a way of expanding as time goes on. So ask for enough so you have a cushion to fall back on. You'll make your life much easier if you ask for at least 10%—and preferably 20%—more than you need! Learn from your author, who has financed many a deal.

Once you know how much money you'll need, you then tell how you'll use the money in the business. Typical approved uses include:

- Buy, or lease, real estate for the firm
- Buy, or lease, machinery and equipment for the firm
- Pay salaries (including yours) of company workers
- Advertise, travel, pay back bills, etc.
- Plus any other business-related expenses

Just be sure to tell it as it is! If you need money to pay back bills the business ran up, state this. Don't hide anything. People who lend you money or invest in your business want to know the whole truth. So tell it!

In helping many BWBs raise millions quickly and easily, one quirk I've seen is this:

- The more bills a business has, the more storms it has passed through, and the more truthful the owners are, the easier—it seems—it is for them to raise the exact amount of money they need! Why is this? Because people who've been through the wringer in business *expect* you to have a few problems. So they try harder to help you by advancing you the funds you need. Crazy—but true.

Once you're finished with the use of the money you'll get, you move into your income and expense estimates. Here's where many people run into trouble. To help you with this part of your plan, I'm giving you two special sections below. Reading those you'll see how easy it is to make your estimates. Let's start!

Figuring Your Future Income

In your business you'll be doing something for money. You might be selling products. Or you might be selling services. Either way, you'll deliver a certain number of items (or hours) at a certain price per item or per hour. To figure your income:

1. *Ask yourself,* how many items or hours will I deliver the first month?
2. *What will be the price* of each item or hour, if all are the same? Or what will be the *average price* of your item or hour, if they're different?
3. *Multiply the count* you have in no. 1 by the price in no. 2. This gives you your first month's income.
4. *Do the same* for each month in the year. Try to see when your sales will increase because of more advertising, greater acceptance, and wider use of your item or hours. Show this in the months you expect it.

YOUR MEDICAL SUPPLIES EXPORT
BUSINESS INCOME ESTIMATES
(Average sales price = $1.25 per unit)

Month No.	No. of Units Exported (= your educated estimate)	Price per Unit	Month's Income (= no. of units x price per unit)
1	12,000	$1.25	$15,000
2	14,000	1.25	17,500
3	16,000	1.25	20,000
4	18,000	1.25	22,500
5	12,000	1.25	15,000
6	14,000	1.25	17,500
7	14,000	1.25	17,500
8	15,000	1.25	18,750
9	18,000	1.25	22,500
10	18,000	1.25	22,500
11	20,000	1.25	25,000
12	22,000	1.25	27,500

Total sales for year = $241,250

Fig. 2-1   *How to estimate your future income in business.*

5. **Add your sales for each month** to give the year's total sales. Do this for each of your first three years in business, and for your fifth year. You now have your projected sales for your business.

To make this method clearer, look at Fig. 2-1. It shows you how to use the above method for an export business. In this business you'll be exporting medical supplies— bandages, gauze, tubing, staples, etc.—having an average sales price of $1.25 per unit. Your estimates of the number of units you'll export each month are given opposite the month number. The number of units will rise and fall with your thoughts as to how demand will change with the seasons of the year.

Note that your estimate of the average price and demand per month is a guess. But it's an educated guess. So it will be close to what really happens when you start your business!

Counting the Costs of Doing Business

It takes money to make money. Everyone knows this. What they mean when they say this is that:

You will usually have costs when you do business. These costs must be paid, if the income—such as that in Fig. 2-1—is to flow into your bank account. So you must know the cost of doing business before you can figure if you'll earn a profit.

Typical costs you're sure to run into in almost any business are these:

Rent for an office, except if you work out of your home
Electricity for lighting your desk, running an electric typewriter, copying machine, etc.
Telephone for making business calls to your customers and suppliers
Postage for letters and packages you send to your customers and suppliers
Supplies of various kinds for any manufacturing you might do, for your office, etc.

Labor for people who do work for your firm and who help you earn a profit
Other costs of various kinds that are unique to the type of business you run.

Again, as with your sales, you make an educated guess as to what your costs will be. There are a number of ways to do this. For example:

- If you're buying a going business, you just use the costs the seller shows you and adjust them, if needed
- If you're in a business that has a trade association, ask them for a listing of the typical costs for a business of the size you have in mind. Use these average costs, adjusting them as needed
- If you're starting your business from scratch, sit down with pencil and paper and estimate how much your rent will run, the cost of electricity, etc. If you do this carefully, you can easily make suitably accurate estimates.

YOUR EXPENSE BUDGET FOR YOUR
MEDICAL SUPPLIES EXPORT BUSINESS

Month No.	Estimated Total Monthly Costs
1	$11,500
2	13,000
3	16,000
4	18,000
5	11,000
6	13,000
7	13,000
8	14,500
9	18,500
10	18,500
11	21,000
12	23,500

Total annual costs = $191,500

Fig. 2-2 *Estimated monthly costs for your business.*

Once you have your estimated costs for your first year in business, break them into monthly costs. The easiest way to do this is to divide each cost by 12 months in the year. This will give you your Expense Budget. The numbers you developed in Fig. 2-1 are called your Sales Budget for your export firm.

To show you how this might work, look at Fig. 2-2. Here we've just added up your total costs for each month and listed them. You would have a separate item for each of your costs—rent, electricity, telephone, etc.—which would add up to the total in Fig. 2-2, for your export business.

Then, to see how much you'll take home every month—which is the whole idea here—set up your Profit Budget, Fig. 2-3. Here you just combine your income from Fig. 2-1 and your costs from Fig. 2-2, and come up with your take-home pay. As you can see, you'll be taking home about $4,000+ each month. Not bad, for your first business!

And remember this—good friend of mine—this $4,000+ per month is *after* your company paid for your:

- *Travel,* if any was needed for the business
- *Auto costs,* if needed for your business

YOUR PROFIT BUDGET FOR YOUR MEDICAL
SUPPLIES EXPORT BUSINESS

Month No.	Month's Income (from Fig. 2-1)	Month's Costs (from Fig. 2-2)	Month's Profit (= income - costs)
1	$15,000	$11,500	$3,500
2	17,500	13,000	4,500
3	20,000	16,000	4,000
4	22,500	18,000	4,500
5	15,000	11,000	4,000
6	17,500	13,000	4,500
7	17,500	13,000	4,500
8	18,750	14,500	4,250
9	22,500	18,500	4,000
10	22,500	18,500	4,000
11	25,000	21,000	4,000
12	27,500	23,500	4,000

Total annual profit = $49,750

Fig. 2-3   *Your Profit Budget.*

- *Hotel,* meals, telephone, etc. for you on business trips
- *Plus any other costs* you might have, including—of course—
your annual salary!

Why Planning Really Works

Planning works because you *think* through your business—
in advance. And, as we've seen so many times, your mind
can make you rich! Your mind *can* make you rich in hundreds
of businesses. Like these, in which *your* plans can put big
money into your pocket:

- *Become a financial broker* and raise money for others—
for a fee. While you're being paid to raise money for other
people, *you* learn the ins and outs of this great business.
Including who's lending for what use. So when you want
to borrow for *your* business, you go to a lender you know
will welcome you. And all this can be done in your spare
time from your home. Your only costs will be pennies for
postage and a telephone! Planning can get you faster results

and bigger commission checks! See the back of this book for information on our great *Fiancial Broker Kit.*

* *Buy income real estate* on a planned basis. Figure out how much profit you'd like to be earning after 1 year, 2 years, 3 years, etc. Then plan on how many buildings or units you'll have to buy to deliver this profit. Use 100% financing (*no* money of your own) to take over each property. Plan which lenders you'll tap for the two loans (at least) you'll need to take over any property—a down-payment loan and a long-term mortgage (which is very easy to get, even with bad credit). Then go out and get the loans you need. See the back of this book for various real-estate kits that can help you get the money you need faster and sooner.

* *Get into the exporting business,* as in the example in this chapter. Exporting is a wonderful business that can be highly profitable. And you can run your entire business by direct mail! You never need to meet a customer, you never need to touch an item you export—you just handle pieces of paper. And you can start with just a few pennies for your postage, plus a few good directories of export opportunities, such as those listed at the back of this book. (I do all my export contacts with the cheapest kind of postage—a 1/2 oz. letter that brings back thousands of dollars every year. To get these cheap rates I use the lightest paper and envelopes and condense all info into just a few pages. You can do the same, too!)

* *Get into direct mail/mail order* in the domestic area. Sell items people need, which they can't get at the local store. Get good lists of prospects for your products and mail to them a fully detailed description of your product and the benefits it offers buyers. Put space ads into magazines— look for each ad to return at least twice what it cost you. If you get three times your cost, you can drive the biggest yacht in your area! I've made many millions in mail order/ direct mail, and I'm ready to share with you my info when you're a subscriber of my newsletter, *International Wealth Success!*

There are hundreds of other good businesses you can get into with the right planning. We'll be looking at these in each chapter in this book.

For now, just keep these key ideas in mind:

- Planning your business *does* make money for you.
- Every business benefits from good planning.
- Your author is here—day and night—to help you with your plans and goals—just call.
- Your mind can make you rich!

DAY 3

With your plan for your future success ready, you are now about to see you dreams fulfilled. What you can see in your mind, you can make true in your life! Your mind can make you rich. And anything is possible for you with an open mind. So today you will visualize— in your mind—your future success. And before long you will see that success taking place in your life. More money will flow into your bank account, better dealings with others will fill your days, and you'll be much happier. With every day of your life a new beginning, you are now ready for the greater success you seek and deserve!

CHAPTER 3

VISUALIZE YOUR ACHIEVEMENTS— AND ENJOY THEM

SUCCESS IS FUN! Why? Because you get to do all those things you dreamed of doing for so many years. Your achievements bring you power and cash that help you do what *you* enjoy!

Use Mental Pictures to Show the Way

Your mind can make you rich—quickly and easily. But to perform its work, your mind must be told what to search for. You—as the controller of your mind—can tell it the goals you seek for your success. How? By using mental pictures of what you want!

When you "see" in your mind the achievements you seek, you bring powerful forces to work for your success. This isn't the place to go into the various theories about how the mind works. Instead, I just want you to use proven ideas that work for millions. Then, after you've reached the success level you seek, you can take time to see why you made it big! For now, I just want you to have the success action program that will help you build a million-dollar fortune for yourself!

To use mental pictures to show you the way to the success you seek, take these easy steps:

1. **Decide** on one aspect of your future success that you'll picture in the next few moments. This could be the filling out of a loan application, an interview for a loan, etc.

2. **"See" yourself** taking the necessary steps to reaching your goal—such as a beautifully typed application, successful loan interview, etc. Do this "seeing" when you have an idle moment, such as walking along the street, waiting for a train, in bed before you go to sleep.

3. **"Feel" and experience**—in your mind—the entire process. Like filling out the application, talking to the loan officer, etc. Say the words you'll use, or write out your answers— all in your mind. See yourself as doing the right thing in each instance. Feel how nice it is to get a *yes* answer to your loan request. Actually "glow" with pride as you realize you did your job well and received the approval you seek.

4. **Repeat your success picture** several times. Don't be satisfied with just one showing! Have a rerun of your success. It will get better every time. Also, your mind will be better prepared to handle the actual real-life situation when it comes about!

5. **Say the words you'll say** if what you're picturing needs words to work. Thus, if you're picturing an interview or seeing yourself making a successful speech to raise money, say the words! Your mind will get used to the words. Your tongue will get used to any difficult words so you don't trip up on them when you actually say them.

Where you have a number of success goals to achieve— and most of us do—make a list of those you want to picture. Then go through each. Check off the ones you've done, as you do them. Thus:

In the many seminars I give around the world, I spend time picturing what I'll say from hour to hour. Then, when I go "on stage" my mind takes over. The words just flow and the audience reacts just the way I imagined it would. My mind is making me rich since the income from such seminars is in the thousands of dollars per day. And the expenses aren't that high! This is one of the best examples of personal experience of the value of mental pictures in showing the way to wealth.

Sometimes you may have trouble picturing your success in your mind. If this happens to you, try using "props"— such as videotapes or movie films. How? Here's a real-life money story of a business friend of mine:

> Jerry T. wanted to raise $500,000 to invest in resort property on a Caribbean island. On my advice, Jerry decided to make a pitch to local doctors and dentists who might be interested in investing with him. But Jerry was poor at making sales pitches. He couldn't "see" himself doing it.
>
> So I advised Jerry to go to his island in the sun and make a videotape (his mental picture) of what he wanted to do with the land and ocean front he would buy with the money he raised.
>
> Jerry took my advice and used his videotape in his pitch to the doctors and dentists. The screen gave him his mind "pictures" and the full-color photos got his message across. All Jerry had to do was talk about the tape as he ran it off. Result? Jerry raised some $700,000 in less than two hours! Truly, your mind can make you rich—anywhere.

Now I know that you may not own a VCR, or a video camera. But these can be rented for a few dollars. Or you can use an audio cassette to practice a talk you'll be giving to get money. You can even borrow a recorder and tape from a relative or friend and it won't cost you anything. What's more, the recorder and tape won't be changed in any way by your use of them!

Keep Your Goals in Front of You Every Day

If you're still having problems with visualizing your goals, try this technique:

1. *Get a photo or drawing* of your goal (or make the drawing yourself), showing exactly what you want, or want to achieve.
2. *Hang, or mount, this picture* in a spot where you'll see it several times a day. One good place to mount your picture is in front of yourself at your desk. Then you'll see it every time you start to work, and while you're working. The picture will spur you on to work harder to get what

you want. And no matter what anyone might tell you, hard work *does* produce the results you see!

3. *Change the picture* as you reach certain goals. Keep putting up new goal pictures to carry yourself ahead as you move forward. When you have a money goal—say $1 million—use that number instead of a picture. You'll find that the number can be just as strong a "pusher" as a picture of an auto, boat, home, etc.

If you travel a lot—to and from work—keep other pictures with you. For those traveling in an auto, you can put a picture or two on the dash. Glance at it when you're stopped for a red light, when you first get into your car, and just before you leave it, after it's safely parked.

Keeping pictures of your success with you every day is very powerful. Thousands of BWBs often write or call me to say:

> "I took your advice and made mental pictures of my future success. It seemed a little crazy when you first suggested it. But I was amazed to see that my real estate business worked out exactly as I had pictured it in my mind. Even the colors of some of the buildings were the same as I pictured them. And the zero-cash deals I pictured worked out almost exactly as I imagined they would. And when I had to make a minor change here or there I was amazed to see that my mind was ready for the change. It almost seemed as if I had been through the deal before. But I really hadn't been—except in my mind. Thanks for pushing me into the "dry-run approach" to business!

Enjoy Your Goals to Achieve Them

Business should be fun to you! Why? For a number of very important reasons. Namely:

- When you're having fun you do a better job and your business prospers.
- Enjoying what you do frees your creativity. So you come up with profitable, money-making ideas.
- Customers react favorably to people who're enjoying themselves—spending more with you.

- Life seems (and is) easier when you're enjoying yourself! Just because you're making money doesn't mean you must have a sorrowful expression on your face every hour of the day. Loosen up and enjoy!

So get back to work on your mental pictures. Even though you're still working toward your goals:

1. *See yourself* enjoying whatever rewards you seek from your business.
2. *Feel the fun* and pleasure of that new sports car, the powerful boat, the sparkling new private plane, the beautiful house you always wanted.
3. *Continue seeing yourself* enjoying what you've worked for. This will reinforce your chances of great success, leading to more achievements in your business.

Look at the executives in large corporations and you'll see a lot of sad-faced people. Why? Because few enjoy what they're doing. And the intense drive for profits forced on them by their bosses takes all the fun out of working. So you'll see a bunch of people whose tails are dragging. They're tired, listless, burned out.

Business owners—by contrast—are often happy, carefree people who have their destiny in their own hands. They make their own decisions. In doing so, they don't have the pressures of a snarling, military-like group above them barking out orders on the number of sales to be made today.

Enjoying—in your mind for now—the results of your work, gives you a great push forward. You want to do more—to enjoy more. So your business gets stronger, bringing *you* greater success! Your mind—as you now know—can make *you* rich. Before you know it, you're achieving the goals you saw as mental pictures in your mind.

See Goals That Put You in Command

We all have goals in life. Some goals are more important than others. For instance:

- A goal of getting a new TV set is a lot less important,

from a business sense, than getting a new delivery van.
- The TV provides—usually—just entertainment. But the delivery van can make money for you.
- And—after all—the goal of every business is to make money!

So start picturing now those goals that will put you in command of money. Why? Because when you command money you have power. You have power over your own life. And—if you wish—you can have power over the lives of others.

Now what kinds of goals will put *you* in command? Here are a number of such goals that will work for almost every Beginning Wealth Builder (BWB). And if they don't work for you, just remember this:

- You can reach me by phone—day or night—and I'll try to help you with *your* goals
- Or, if you don't like talking on the phone, you can write me in care of my newsletter, and I'll help you free of any charge if you're a two-year, or longer, subscriber. You *do* have a friend in Ty Hicks!

Here's a listing of business goals that work for most BWBs:

1. Get the money you need.
2. Control an income producer.
3. Find suitable workers for your business.
4. Expand your business—if you wish.
5. Rake in the wealth.

Let's take a look at each of these goals and see how you can use it to build your wealth. We do want to make you rich—soon!

Get the Money You Need

In every business you need money to earn money. Some businesses need just a small amount of money. Others need large amounts. If your business is a new one, or if it offers a big chance for enormous profits, consider getting venture capital—money that never need be repaid.

You can get venture capital from various sources. Many of my readers regularly raise venture capital from:

- *Private sources*—people with excess funds who want to see their money grow without working in a business every day.
- *Venture-capital firms*—companies organized to provide money for new and growing firms that promise strong growth in an important industry.
- *Venture-capital funds*—usually limited partnerships put together to invest money in promising firms that will grow quickly and reward investors with an increase in the value of their money.

Today, you can often get venture capital on the basis of a simple Executive Summary (Chapter 2) and a short business plan. Some private venture investors will even put up money just on the basis of a good Executive Summary. To contact any of the three types of venture-capital investors listed above, take these easy steps:

1. *Look locally* in your "Yellow Pages" and similar business listings under the category "Venture Capital."
2. *Contact* each firm and ask (by phone or mail) if they're interested in seeing your Executive Summary for a _____ business?
3. *If you get a yes answer,* send your Executive Summary immediately. Wait for a response.
4. *Should the venture capitalist* ask for a business plan, supply it immediately.
5. *Keep trying* until you find a venture capitalist who's interested in your deal.

One of my readers asked me to recommend a venture capitalist who would fund $5 million for a ski lodge. Here's what happened:

I gave the reader the name and phone number of one of my good venture-capital friends. The reader called him and was told: "We just did one of those deals; so we're out of that field for now. But go see Mr. 'A.' He likes ski lodges." The reader called Mr. "A" and was told much the same. But he was also told to call Mr. "B." He struck out with Mr. "B" but was told to call Mr. "C," which he did. Sure enough, Mr. "C" provided the $5 million the reader needed. So he

got the money—even though it took some calling and hard
work.

What all of this shows is that you can benefit from every
contact you make with private sources, venture-capital firms,
and venture funds. And the more contacts you make, the
greater your chances of getting the money you seek.

Where large sums of venture capital are needed—say
$500,000 and up—I use a group of New York venture firms
that I've known for years. These 25 firms account for many
millions in deals every year. And they can be relied on to
give quick answers in a highly professional way.

If you'd like help with the names and addresses of venture-
capital firms that might help you, try the *Venture Capital
Millions Kit,* listed at the back of this book. It can get you
started getting venture money for your business!

Another way to raise money for your new business is to
get people to lend you money that you'll invest in income
producers that pay a high return. Here's a good example
of this way to raise money:

1. *Say you're interested* in owning income real estate of some
   kind. But you don't have the down payment money needed.
2. *You get investors* to lend you money in small (or large)
   amounts—say $5,000 or $10,000 per investor. You promise
   each investor a high interest rate on his or her money.
   For instance, you could promise a 13% interest rate when
   the going Certificate of Deposit (CD) rate is 7%. Money
   will pour into your business because people want those
   high returns!
3. *Once you have the money* you need, you buy the income
   properties that will give the return you've promised your
   investors. To be sure you deliver what you've promised,
   you should seek a return *higher* than the promised number.
   Thus, if you promise 13%, you should get an actual return
   of 15%, or more. Then you'll be sure to deliver what you
   promised. Better yet, your investors will tell their friends:
   "I'm working with this brilliant real-estate operator who
   pays me exactly what was promised—a rate that's much
   higher than any CD." The investor's friends will ask for

your name and phone number so they can send you money
to invest for them!
4. **When you sell the income producer,** repay the money
you've borrowed (called the *principal*) to your investors.
And if your profit on the sale is high, consider paying
your investors a little more than they loaned you. This
is called an *equity kicker.* And investors love those extra
bucks you pay them. Again—they'll tell their friends—
with the same results as mentioned above.

To borrow money this way is easy. Why? Because you don't
have to issue stock. So there are no regulations to contend
with. And a loan is *not* a security. So it's easy to set up the
funding. Just be certain to have a local attorney guide you
in setting up your company. The cost is well worth it since
you avoid potential headaches. Call your firm a *mortgage
fund.* Why?

Because a *mortgage fund,* when used for real estate, can
raise tremendous amounts of money for you. One firm using
this method raised more than $1 billion for real-estate use.
So we're talking big bucks when we think of mortgage funds.
(For 42 ways to get regular loans, see Fig. 3-1).

Taken with venture capital, which—in a recent year—put
out $2.3 billion, mortgage funds can really put *you* in the
chips! Try one and see for yourself.

Get Your Income Source Under Control

Getting the money is your first step. But it really is not
the end of the road! The purpose of the money is to get
control of an income source or producer. What kinds of sources
are we talking about? Here are just a few sources that can
produce big bucks for you:

• Income real estate of many different types
• A going import-export business
• Manufacturing businesses of all types
• Retail businesses such as stores, malls, shopping centers
• Mail-order/direct-mail businesses
• Publishing and information-based businesses
• Money businesses—small loan companies, credit repair, etc.

Fig. 3-1 42 Ways to Get Business Loans

Here are 42 ways to get regular business loans for your fortune-building ideas. If you have any questions on any of these ways, just contact your author. You can find moneylenders in these ways:

1. Check ads in your local paper under "Capital Available."
2. Look under "Funds/Funding Available" in your *IWS** newsletter.
3. Look for "Money Available" ads in industry magazines and newspapers.
4. Write, or call, local or national banks. Ask for loan info.
5. Write, or call, local or national finance companies. Ask for loan info.
6. Write, or call, local or national mortgage companies. Ask for loan info.
7. Write, or call, local or national credit unions. Ask for loan info.
8. Write, or call, local savings & loan associations (S&Ls).
9. Write, or call, local building & loan associations (B&Ls).
10. Run classified ads (free to subscribers) in *IWS* for "Lenders Wanted."
11. Run classified ads in national papers seeking lenders.
12. Co-broker with financial brokers having lenders available.
13. Contact local and national real-estate brokers.
14. Work with franchisors who can supply lenders for buyers.
15. Work with equipment lease brokers having contacts with lenders.
16. Explore overseas lenders through local branch offices.
17. Check federal government loans—there are hundreds available.
18. Contact your state or city government for loans—there are many.
19. Use credit card lines of credit as loan sources.
20. Get finders to locate suitable loans for you.
21. Seek out private lenders among business associates.
22. Work with big-ticket item funders for boats, planes, etc.
23. Contact insurance companies for large real-estate loans.
24. Work with surety-bond firms, using lenders acceptable to them.

---

* *IWS* is the abbreviation for *International Wealth Success*, the monthly newsletter published by the author.

(Fig. 3-1 Continued)

25. Attend lender meetings to get an inside track on their loan needs.
26. Contact local professionals (MDs, DDSs) seeking investments.
27. Write or call attorneys and accountants, asking for lender names.
28. Contact large firms making loans to suppliers.
29. Ask stockbrokers for clients who want to make loans.
30. Get business associates to take out home equity loans.
31. Ask you bank to recommend other lenders to you.
32. Deal with specialty lenders—ship, aircraft, truck, etc.
33. Work with nonprofit lenders—see your "Yellow Pages" for names.
34. Get loans from SBICs — Small Business Investment Companies.
35. Contact local business development companies.
36. Borrow on the cash value of an insurance policy.
37. Apply to pension funds for large real-estate loans.
38. Get accounts receivable financing (AR) from AR lenders.
39. Borrow on commercial paper you issue through your corporation.
40. Use a banker's acceptance (BA) to get import-export loans. See your bank.
41. Get venture-capital firms to lend money to your company.
42. Get loans from tax-haven lenders—usually banks.

- Consulting businesses for large and small firms
- Service businesses of many types—personnel agencies, cleaning services, machinery repair, etc.
- Entertainment businesses—tennis courts, billiard rooms, videotape rental, etc.

You can *control* an income source in two ways: (1) You can lease it and collect the income, or (2) you can buy it and have the complete income for yourself. Of the two ways to control an income source, owning it is the best. Why? Because when you own a business:

1. You're fully in control. You make the decisions and you reap the rewards of smart management.

2. As your business grows, so too does its worth and the value of your investment. If you improve a leased business, the only person who really benefits is the owner—not you!

To get control of an income source, you have to find it. But before you find it you must decide:

1. What type of income source you seek
2. See the list above for typical successful sources for BWBs.

Once you know what type of income source you want, you're ready to start looking for it. To find good sources:

1. Look in your local papers under "Businesses for Sale."
2. Look in the *IWS* newsletter under "Business Opportunities."
3. Contact local business brokers; ask for their free lists of businesses for sale.
4. Check with any trade association in the field of the business; such associations often have lists of businesses for sale.

Get yourself a small notebook as soon as you start your search. Use this notebook to keep a record of:

• Name, address, and telephone number of each business you check out
• Income and expenses of each business
• Asking price of the business, plus the amount of cash down payment requested
• Any interesting facts about the business, its owner, or its personnel.

Once you get enough information on several businesses, sketch out a rough comparison of them, as shown in Fig. 3-2. Having such a listing will quickly tell you a lot about each business, such as:

• Total income
• Total expenses
• Asking price vs. income
• Profit you might expect.

Many of my BWB readers who've prepared tables like that in Fig. 3-2 call me up to say:

Fig. 3-2

Business Buyer's Comparison Chart.

Type of Business: Video Rental and Sales Store

Store	Annual Sales	Annual Expenses	Net Profit	Total Asking Price	Cash Down Payment	Notes
A	$150,000	$125,000	$25,000	$300,000	$60,000	In business less than 1 yr
B	326,000	280,000	46,000	450,000	90,000	Has club with 5,000 members
C	192,000	160,000	32,000	360,000	36,000	Owner ill; forced sale
D	266,000	212,000	54,000	435,000	80,000	Lots of competition in area

Contact data:

Store	Seller	Address	Telephone No.
A	J Smith	123 Elm St	123-4567
B	A Jones	456 Oak St	321-9876
C	C Block	987 Fir St	876-2345
D	Y Crane	432 Pine St	333-4444

You won't believe this, Ty, but I'm now an expert on the _____ business. Talking to sellers and getting all that info you suggested really clued me in on this business! I'm even thinking of becoming a consultant to help others who're thinking of getting into the business. Thanks for suggesting that I do this. It was easier than I thought it would be. And it really paid off since I knew what price to offer the seller. I got the best deal that anyone in the business ever go—thanks to you!

Once you've decided which of several businesses you want to control, make an offer on it. When making your offer, remember the Hicks rule of buying any business:

- Never pay the asking price! Always offer less than the asking price. The seller expects to be "knocked down" on the selling price. So the asking price has always been raised to reflect this. If you pay the asking price, the seller will only think of you as inexperienced and naive! Again— NEVER PAY THE ASKING PRICE—you can always get the business for less!

If you're starting a business from scratch, there won't be an asking price. But you still can negotiate items such as:

- Rent for an office
- Prices of equipment—copiers, typewriters, computers, and other similar machines
- Lease arrangements for expensive machines.

The whole key is to see that you can get almost anything for less! Why? Because when you have the money, you're in command! So exert that command now, when you're just starting your business. Such a view will almost ensure your great success in everything you do.

To help yourself negotiate better, visualize talking to suppliers. Hear the words you'll say. If you can, speak these words out loud in the privacy of your room. Say your "piece" several times. You'll find that you'll gain confidence each time you do.

And remember this:

The methods of visualization we suggest here work for every business! All business people are alike when it comes to deals. So if you learn to wheel and deal (negotiate) you can do it for any business that interests you. And this skill will remain with you for life. It can save you (and make you) millions in a short time!

Now that you've bought or started your income source and have it under control, you're ready to make big money. Let's see how!

Find Suitable Workers for Your Business

No matter what business you're in, you'll need help of some kind. You can't do everything yourself! And you shouldn't have to do everything—if you do, the business isn't being managed right. Remember that! To find suitable workers take these steps:

1. Look first among your relatives. Many of the people in your family might make good part- or full-time workers. Consider both young and not-so-young relatives. One of my best workers is an 84-year-old man who outproduces every younger person on the staff! And you'll find that 8-year-olds love to run copying machines and do a great job, too.
2. Next, look to friends. Many will be happy to work for you. You can get them interested just by telling them about your business. And good friends will often have excellent suggestions for improving your business.
3. Now look to business associates who might need work. Many will have skills that will help your business. Get these people to work for you by telling them about your business. Then ask: "Do you know anyone who might be interested in working for us?" Often, your friend will reply: "Did you ever think of hiring me?" Your ready answer is: "Sure, but I didn't know if you'd be interested!" A person hired on this basis often makes a loyal and talented employee.
4. Lastly, look to employment agencies and newspaper and magazine ads. While these sources can help you find suitable people, the best sources are the first three above.

When you hire anyone, I suggest that you do so on a free-lance basis. Why? For a number of reasons:

1. Your cost will be lower. With a freelancer you don't have any benefits (health, pension, and dental coverage) to pay. So your cost for any employee who's a freelancer will be at least 22% less than for a full-time employee.
2. You can get to know a freelancer without making a promise of a regular job. If the freelancer doesn't work out, then you can just stop offering work to the person. You don't have to go through the painful process of firing someone.
3. Freelancers work harder than regular employees. Why? For a number of reasons. These reasons are: Freelancers need the money; so they work harder. And many of these people would like to get a permanent job. So they work harder

to impress you, hoping that you'll hire them on a permanent basis.

4. Using freelancers frees you of the painful job of meeting a weekly payroll. You pay freelancers *only* when they work. So you're not faced with a heavy payroll just at the time that your firm has only a little cash on hand. You move ahead without strain!

Freelancers help me make millions. And they can do the same for you. But the benefits are not all one-sided. My freelancers have:

- Put kids through college on their earnings from me
- Bought new cars and new homes with their earnings
- Learned many new skills using equipment in my business.

At the same time, I've reaped many benefits from these freelancers. For example:

- Our 84-year-old worker regularly brings in from $1,000 to $2,000 in sales each week. And he tries to keep upping the sales every week.
- A 36-year-old housewife opens our mail and counts the income every day. She's accurate, reliable, and completely honest. Paid by the hour, only when she works, she frees me up to concentrate on new money-making products that will make all of us rich. She even makes bank deposits of our income.

Get the right people for your business and you're sure to be successful. Why? Because the right people make your customers feel better. So people spend more with you. These right people give you more time to make more money. And making money *is* the name of this game!

Expand Your Business—If You Wish

Every business must grow if it is to survive. In a business if you don't grow in sales, you're moving backwards. So you have to expand your business just to keep up with the changes going on all around you.

Expanding a business is easy—if you know how. Here are a number of proven ways to expand any business today:

1. Get new products to sell. The life of any business depends on its products. Unless you offer your customers new products on a regular basis, your business will almost certainly decline. Why is this? Because people seek the new. They want new items to help them do something, earn more money, etc. By offering new products, you expand your business.

2. Make your products or services so they help people solve a problem of some kind. Then your customers will have good reasons to buy what you offer. While you can make a fortune selling silly items, you'll get a lot richer if you sell something that really helps people cope with life better. During your search for new products, keep in mind the idea of products that solve problems—and your money problems will be solved forever!

3. Look around to see if there are other firms you can take over for little or no money. This is called *acquisition,* and it can expand your business enormously. You can easily double or triple your sales just by taking over one other firm. I suggest that you look first for firms in a similar business. Why? Because taking over another firm in a different business can be hard when you're first starting out. Later, after you have some experience, you can consider buying firms in different businesses, or *diversifying.*

4. Expand your advertising so you reach more prospects. Effective ads *will* sell more for you. Expand your ad coverage by getting free publicity for your products or services. Publicity often makes more sales than advertising. But you need both! One won't do the entire job for you. So get all the publicity you can—it really pays off in more sales!

To show you how these methods work, I'd like to give you a few real-life examples from my own business. As you may know I've published my newsletter, *International Wealth Success,* for more than 23 years. When I started it in the small study of my home, I had only one product—the newsletter. But as time went on I:

- Started publishing books related to the content of the newsletter that would appeal to its subscribers.
- Introduced 10 kits covering financial brokerage, mail order, real estate, import-export, etc. Each kit is priced at $99.50.

- Branched out into credit card publishing to help people with their credit problems.
- Developed 8 new specialized kits priced at $100 each, targeted at current real-estate, loan, venture-capital, and similar problems.

The result of all this has been increased income and profits. Had I just stayed with one newsletter, I'm sure I'd be struggling along with hardly any income. And readers often call to say:

> Thanks for telling me to expand. My income is now five times what it was when I first called you. In fact, my new business is so strong, I've almost given up my first business! But that was the business that allowed me to buy the second. So I keep it going because it really opened a whole new world to me. Thanks so much for your help in this office-cleaning business.

And

> I always thought that if I could get a business that gave me $100,000 a year, I'd be happy. But when I bought a small shopping center that gave me that much income, after all expenses including mortgage payments, I quickly realized that I had to expand my business. Why? Well, there were a number of malls in the area that were putting in new stores like crazy. If I didn't expand, the shops in my small center could start losing business. In a year or so, they'd move elsewhere. This would leave me with vacant stores and my income would go down. So I started expanding—borrowing money to improve and enlarge my center. It really paid off because I was able to sell the center two years later and buy a huge mall giving me an income three time as large! You can't resist expanding a business—unless you want to go into a slow decline. That's something I avoid every day of the week!

Rake in the Wealth

Once you have your business up and running you're ready to rake in the wealth. How? By taking these easy steps:

1. Keep improving your products or services.

2. Pay attention to what customers tell you.
3. Try to act on sensible customer suggestions.
4. Cut costs to the minimum; maximize your profits.
5. Watch your business—every day.
6. Keep accurate income and expense records.
7. Never let costs get out of control; stop spending altogether until you know where the money is going.
8. Use "Top Line Management"—that is, get the sales. If the money is coming in, I'm sure you can manage your costs so you take home more profits. But without the sales, there's little you can do to increase profits.

Visualize your staff making big sales. See them receiving money from customers every day. Ask your staff to visualize themselves making sales. Tell them to feel—in their minds— the glow of success from each sale. Then watch the sales being made!

You can use your visualization magic in any type of business. Here are six wealth-building businesses where I've seen people turn their mental pictures into millions. You can do the same—and build *your* million-dollar fortune— using your mind to make yourself rich!

1. **Start a high-priced service** for people who need some special information or service. Thus, one friend of mine publishes a newsletter for banks that's priced at $3,600 per year. With only 1,000 subscribers (not a very large number) he can bring in $3,600,000 a year! Since his costs are low, his profit is very high. What kind of service can you render that can be priced high and will be valuable to customers? If you can corner a bit of information, or a service, that's valuable to people, you can make a million-dollar fortune in just months!

2. **Start a franchise company** that can sell your ideas, or the ideas of others, to people who want to go into business for themselves. Thus, you can get a franchise fee of anywhere from $5,000 to $50,000, or more, for an idea that will make a profitable business. Since your costs are low, your profits will be high. Thus, if you sell 50 franchises a year at $10,000 each, your total income will be $500,000. Not bad for just dealing in ideas!

3. **Become a loan packager** and put together loan deals for businesses needing cash. Charges for packaging loan

applications can range from $750 to as high as $25,000, depending on how much work must be done. All you need to do this work is a typewriter and some paper. Or if you'd prefer to do venture-capital deals, you can use the *Venture Capital Millions Kit*, listed at the back of this book. It shows *you* how to make big money preparing Executive Summaries and business plans for firms seeking venture capital—money that never need be repaid. Again, all you need is a typewriter and some paper. Your income can exceed $100,000 a year in either business.

4. ***Get the rights to out-of-print books*** from publishers. All you need do is write a simple letter asking for the rights. Once you get the rights, reprint the books and sell them at high prices. You can charge a high price for such books because people know the books are not available in any other form. With an active reprint program going, your income potential can be in the many millions.

5. ***Become an invention marketer***—that is, help people sell their inventions to a large company or other buyer. You're paid a fee for each invention you consider. Then, if more work is needed to market the invention, you are paid an additional fee. And—if you wish—you can ask for a share in the royalties from the invention, after it is sold. Such royalties can bring you really large dollars—millions— if the invention catches on. And you need just one of these inventions to set you up for life!

6. ***Rent desirable real estate*** and then sublet it to others at a rental that's higher than what you're paying! Use a net-net-net lease where your client pays *all* costs above the rent. Your income is the difference between what you're paid and what you pay. Get $1 per year per sq. ft. over your cost and your income rises as you put more square footage under lease. Thus, at $1 per sq. ft. 500,000 sq. ft. will give you an income of $500,000 a year; 1-million sq. ft. = $1 million per year! Not bad when you do it just with paper—you don't even own one brick in the building!

Yes, you can visualize your achievements and enjoy them to build a million-dollar fortune. And the sooner you start to see your achievements—and enjoy then—the sooner they'll become reality in your life.

Just remember: You have a friend in your author. I'm here to help you with ideas, advice, experience, and financing. Using these services, I'm almost certain that you *can* build your million-dollar fortune—using your mind. Just remember—at all times—*Your mind can make you rich!* Isn't it about time that you started seeing those riches and then taking action to make them yours?

DAY 4

Much of your success depends on your outlook on yourself and your business. If you have a Rich Mental Attitude (RMA), you will be able to Understand, Act, *and* Obtain. *Thus, you'll understand what you have to do, you'll act on this understanding, and you'll obtain what you seek. So turn the page to learn how to develop a RMA that can help you build your million-dollar fortune—soon!*

CHAPTER 4

ADOPT A RICH MENTAL ATTITUDE—AND BANK THE RESULTS

HAVING A RICH MENTAL ATTITUDE (RMA, I call it) can get you fast results in all your million-dollar fortune building. I see this every day of the week. So I kid you not when I say:

- Having a Rich Mental Attitude can carry you far in your wealth search
- Helping you overcome fear, shyness, and other problems that can hold you back from success
- And giving you the results you seek—sooner and with less work than you might ever think!

So What Is a Rich Mental Attitude?

A Rich Mental Attitude (RMA) is a state of mind in which you:

> *Look at the positive aspects of every money and business situation so you understand it better, take action when action is needed, and strive for the best from yourself and others. Your RMA helps you* Understand, Act *and* Obtain!

Let me give you an example of a BWB's RMA in action and the results it gets. As most of my readers know, I'm president and chairman of the board of a large lending organization. Also, I have my own lending firm, IWS, Inc., which makes business and real-estate loans to my newsletter readers, and others. Often, here's what happens when a BWB with an RMA subscribes to our newsletter for two years or longer:

- The BWB calls me on the phone and says: "I need a business loan for $100,000 and I don't have time to wait for a lot of loan approvals. I'm sure this deal will do well. It will repay your loan way ahead of time. What should I send you to get approval?"
- My answer is short—"Send me info on the sales and profits you expect, the amount of the loan you need, and how long it will take to repay it."
- With this, the BWB with the RMA rattles off the numbers. This really impresses me because anyone who has enough guts to think through a project this way will really make it hum! Result? The BWB with the RMA usually gets his or her loan—*fast!*

While an RMA gets some BWBs their money faster, what might it do for you, a BWB who—possibly—does not need money? You'll find that if you adopt a RMA that:

- You get more done in less time.
- You *act*, instead of just dreaming.
- Your knowledge of business grows fast.

Thousands of BWBs tell me they zoomed their wealth by taking on a RMA. Here are just a few who recently went from flat broke (or nearly so) to the Million Dollar Fortune status:

- A large-city BWB was able to talk the seller of a $1.2-million apartment house into selling it to him for zero cash down! How? By convincing the seller that he is a sincere, hard-working real-estate wealth builder who sees himself as a multimillionaire. The building has a positive cash flow— every month.
- Three electronics engineers founded their own firm with the belief they could raise $3 million to get their business going. With a RMA on the part of each engineer, they were able to convince a venture-capital firm to invest $3

million in their new company, even though they didn't have a cent in sales yet. These engineers started their company in September and by November of the same year they had their $3 million. And by the following June they raised another $8 million—all based on a belief in what they could get their new company to do in the marketplace! Nice results for their RMA.

Remember—most people in this life are *downers*—they see nothing but the negative side of things. This is why almost everyone fails to really do big things with his or her life. For example, a downer will tell you:

- Nothing works for me—I tried everything but nothing worked.

But a person with a RMA says:

- Everything I try works out. Sometimes it takes a little longer but I do succeed in what I do!

Build a Million-Dollar Fortune on Your RMA

You can adopt your RMA this instant—at no cost at all! It won't cost you a penny but it may make you a millionaire. A good example of this is my reader, Ken D. Here's his real-life experience:

Ken was a downer until we spoke. He asked for some advice and when I offered it, he told me "Oh, I tried that and it doesn't work!" My fast response was "OK, Ken, I'm hanging up because I know that the next item I suggest you will have already tried and found it doesn't work. I don't deal with downers!" With that I hung up.

Ken called me back and said he was sorry. "What can I do to change?" he asked. I told him that he'd have to adopt a Rich Mental Attitude. And I outlined what I meant by that—namely, Think Rich, Act Rich, Look Rich, and You'll be Rich in your chosen field.

Ken took my advice and went into financial brokerage to get loans for small companies in his area. He knew they needed money badly and he chose a new way to approach local banks. Instead of bringing in one loan application at a time, Ken decided to bring in ten. With these ten he brought people from each company and they all made a presentation about their firm to the bank officers. The idea was welcomed by the bank since it saved a lot of time for everyone. And time—you know—is money! Especially to bankers.

To save money, Ken presented his ideas to the local Rotary and other business groups. Before he knew it, he was flooded with loan applications. To help with his costs, Ken charged each company a modest consulting fee of $250. The companies were pleased to pay Ken since his ideas were so original.

Ken was soon getting large loans for many of his clients. And with each presentation he made, Ken improved on his ideas. Thus, he went from a slide presentation to movies to a videotape description of the company, in full color, to plant visits by the bankers.

To attract more lenders to his business, Ken used some of the 30 methods shown in Fig. 4-1. These really paid off for him in new clients. He set a sales target of closing at least one loan a week and getting one new client every business day.

In his first year of going from a downer to someone with a healthy RMA, Ken went from just $12,000 a year to an independent income of more than $100,000. His RMA really paid off. Today Ken's income is several times that of his first year's. And he's a very happy BWB who's in full control of his life and future! All because he's using a RMA toward his chosen work. He expects to have his million-dollar fortune very soon!

Fig. 4-1   *Thirty Ways to Find Money Borrowers.*

Here are 30 ways to find money borrowers who might pay you fees for helping them find the financing they seek. Use the ways you like.

1. Run classified ads in local papers under "Capital Available."
2. Answer classified or space ads run by people seeking money.
3. Contact real-estate brokers for names of buyers (or sellers) needing money.
4. Contact business brokers for names of people needing money.

Fig. 4-1 *Continued*

5. Tell your friends and business associates that you can find money.
6. Contact venture-capital firms for names of rejects.
7. Contact banks for names of loan rejects.
8. Contact auto dealers for names of loan rejects.
9. Contact small finance companies for reject names.
10. Contact franchise companies for applicants needing money.
11. Contact "For Sale by Owner" sellers for names of possible borrowers.
12. Contact stockbrokers for names of clients needing money.
13. Contact boat sales agencies for names of people needing money.
14. Check aircraft sales agents for names of people needing money.
15. Contact lease brokers for names of people needing down payment money.
16. Advertise free of charge in the *IWS** newsletter for people seeking money.
17. Contact unions for names of members needing money.
18. Check with doctors and dentists for names of patients needing money.
19. Contact health professionals who may need money—many do!
20. Check with hospitals for people who owe money.
21. Contact attorneys for names of people owing money.
22. Check with factoring companies for names of firms needing money.
23. Check with credit unions for their loan reject names.
24. Contact mortgage companies for names of people needing money.
25. Check with collection agencies for names of people needing money.

*IWS *is the shortened name for the newsletter,* **International Wealth Success,** *published by the author.*

26. Contact credit-card issuers for bad-debt names.
27. Check with banks and credit unions for names of their deadbeats.
28. Ask department stores for names of needy borrowers.
29. Find private lenders and ask for names of deadbeats.
30. Get names of debtors from gas-card and department-store-card issuers.

Note: The motivation for providing you names of debtors, is the payment of a debt or the sale of the item. This will often be enough for the creditor to reveal the name and address to you. In providing money you are helping everyone.

How to Combine Your RMA with Business Success

You can follow a few simple rules to combine your RMA with business and money success. (If real estate is your "thing," remember that it's a business—just like any other. So these rules apply to real estate, also). To combine money success and your RMA:

1. Seek new ways to solve a pressing problem. (Ken found a new way to save time for banks while getting money for local firms needing it. And by combining ten applications in one presentation, Ken showed he was working to save work by the banks.)
2. Devise a low-cost way to promote your idea. (Ken goes to Rotary and other business meetings and gets his service known just by talking to people. He doesn't even have to pay for lunch because people are glad to have him there to talk about getting them money.)
3. Earn an immediate income for yourself. (Ken does this by means of his consulting fee—which the small firms are happy to pay. Why? Ken brings an expert opinion on their money problems to them. *Note:* This is *not* an "advance fee" payment. Instead, it is a fair, and reasonable, consulting fee.)
4. Set a sales target for yourself. (Ken does this by trying to close one loan a week and by getting one new client a day. You can have similar goals for yourself, if you wish.)
5. Improve on your basic idea as often as you can. By making your idea better each time, you increase sales. (Ken does

this by changing how he presents information to his prospective lenders.)
6. Seek new ideas for your business every day. Be an idea person. Your mind can make you rich! And your RMA will give you the drive to make your ideas make you big money. (Ken is doing this, increasing his income every year by expanding to new markets.)
7. Build your RMA *every* day. By thinking rich, looking rich, and acting rich, you *will* become rich! That I can almost guarantee—for you. Setting your mind to the goal you seek unlocks great power within yourself. Before you know it, what you seek so strongly becomes reality in your life. It did in Ken's and it can—I'm sure—in your life!

Treat Yourself to Riches—Use OPM

Once Ken became successful he found that lenders began to pester him to invest money for them. He had millions of dollars of Other People's Money (OPM, I call it) available to him. Why? Because he:

- Knew *who* needed money for business or real estate
- Could judge these potential borrowers quickly
- Was ready to recommend good borrowers
- Built up a good track record of repaid loans.

You can get access to millions of dollars of OPM, also. This money can make money for you. Or you can use it as a source of money for your own business deals. Either way, money will flow into your bank because of your RMA and what you do.

Here are four ways for you to control OPM and make money from it. Each way has its own unique features that may appeal to you. Hundreds of my readers make money from each of these ways every day. So I'm ready to help you do the same. Just follow my guides and you'll soon have that million-dollar fortune you seek! These ways to control OPM are:

1. Become a lease broker for business equipment.

2. Handle mortgage cashout deals for real estate.
3. Get loans for health professionals.
4. Help small and minority businesses get loans.

Let's take a look at each of these ways to control OPM and see if you like it. If you do, you're off and running toward *your* million-dollar fortune!

Become a Lease Broker

Lease brokers bring together a person or business wanting to lease a piece of business equipment and the firm that leases this item. For this service the lease broker earns a commission from the company that supplies the leased equipment. The types of equipment you might handle include:

- Personal computers
- Telephone systems
- Typewriters
- Automobiles, trucks
- Machine tools
- Store fixtures
- Copying machines
- Satellite antennas
- Office furniture
- Construction equipment
- Farm equipment
- Medical and dental equipment

Now don't let the names of the equipment types scare you! Why? Well, you do't really have to know anything about the equipment to be a lease broker. You just bring the renter of the equipment together with the firm that supplies the equipment.

You will usually earn a 4% commission on each lease. This means that you will get paid amounts like those below for various leases:

COST OF LEASED EQUIPMENT, $	YOUR COMMISSION AT 4% OF COST, $
100,000	4,000
500,000	20,000
1,000,000	40,000
5,000,000	200,000

Now what do you do for commissions of these amounts? The answer is simple. You:

1. Find firms seeking to lease some equipment—for example, laser printers are very popular rental items today because their prices are higher than many small firms want to lay out. You can find such firms by running short classified ads such as these:

   > Lease any business equipment for a low monthly fee. Call 123-4567.

   Or:

   > Need expensive business equipment? Save money— lease what you need. Call 123-4567.

2. Have the firm fill out the lease application. This is a simple 3-page application that tells about the firm and what it wants to lease or rent. You should have this application typed since this makes a much better impression on the lender.
3. Send, or bring, the lease application to the firm that does the leasing. You will have your answer in just hours. And your commission will be paid by the company that supplies the equipment—called the lessor. So you don't have to worry about being paid. You get your money fast!

You can learn more about leasing from the leasing kits described at the back of this book. Each kit supplies you with the needed forms, plus many lessors ready to work with you. With a little work, leasing could build *your* million-dollar fortune! Try it and see for yourself.

Handle Mortgage Cashout Deals

Many people who sold real estate using "creative financing" would like to take their cash out of the deal. Why? Because cash in hand is more valuable to most people than a future stream of payments. Here's a good example of this:

> John T. sold his home for $500,000. But the buyer could not come up with the $150,000 cash needed after the 70% first mortgage issued by a local bank put $350,000 into the property. The most the buyer could come up with was $50,000. So John T. "took back" a $100,000 seven-year mortgage from

the buyer in order to sell the house and move elsewhere.

Two years later, John T. needed some money for tuition for one of his children. But the income from his mortgage was only $1,765.28 a month. John needed a fast $12,000. That's when he thought to himself: "Maybe I could sell that mortgage and take cash out of it and pay this $12,000 tuition bill in full." This is where a person like yourself would come into action.

In handling mortgage cashout deals you just shuffle a few pieces of paper. Here's what you do:

   1. You place small classified ads saying:

Need cash? We buy mortgages anywhere. Call 123-4567.

Or:

Take cash out of your purchase-money mortgage. We'll buy any mortgage. Call 123-4567.

   2. Once someone calls, get the info on their mortgage. The data you need are simple. They are:

- Amount of mortgage
- Interest rate borrower pays
- Number of months remaining on the mortgage
- Monthly payment amount
- Number of monthly payments made by the borrower.

   3. With this info in hand you send it to a mortgage buyer. If the buyer accepts the mortgage for purchase (and almost all *are* accepted) you get a 4% fee from the lender. The seller of the mortgage (John T. in the above case) gets from 65% to 75% of the amount still owed on the mortgage. While this is less than he would get if he waited out the full repayment, he has cash-in-hand—*now!* And that's what almost everyone wants today—cash in hand.

You can get all you need to know to start in this wonderful paper business by reading a few good books on mortgages. If you want specific help, including a lender who works with brokers like yourself, see the *Discount Mortgage Broker's Cashout Kit* listed at the back of this book. And *no* license is needed to be successful in this business—especially if you combine it with your RMA! It's an ideal paper business.

Get Loans for Health Professionals

Health professionals of all types—doctors, dentists, optometrists, chiropractors, etc.—often need money in the form of a loan. Why? They seem to run up bills faster than most folks. You can build your million-dollar fortune serving the needs of these important people.

Why don't they just go to their local bank, you ask. For a number of very good reasons, such as:

1. They're loaned up at the local bank.
2. They've been slow payers to the bank on other loans.
3. The bank doesn't have any more money to loan out now.

You can come to the aid of these health professionals. How? By offering them loans of various types, such as:

- Unsecured signature loans up to $60,000 each, with *no* loan fees of any kind and a $1,000 fee to you on each loan after it is granted.
- Accounts receivable loans where the health professional receives immediate payment for services rendered to a patient without having to wait.
- Sale and leaseback of equipment, giving the health professional immediate cash-in-hand while having use of the same equipment to which he or she is accustomed.
- 20-year amortization (payoff) loans for any purpose the health professional may choose. Amounts range from $50,000 to $1.2 million per borrower.

Handling loans like these can put you on the fast-track to your million-dollar fortune sooner than you think. Why spend years slaving for a penny-pinching company at coolie wages when you can get into the lucrative field of handling loans for health professionals? Again, you only handle pieces of paper.

To find lenders who like health professionals as clients, watch the ads in your local newspaper. Sooner or later you'll probably see an ad from a lender who wants to work with health personnel of all kinds. Contact the lender immediately and tell a loan officer that you want to represent the lender to health professionals. If you do, you're on your way!

As an alternate source of funding, you can use the lender with whom I deal. Full details are given in the *4 Doctor Loan Programs* described at the end of this book.

Help Small and Minority Businesses Get Loans

There are millions of small businesses in the United States needing loans. Many of these small firms are run by minorities. You can make your million-dollar fortune helping either—or both—types of firms get the loans they need.

When a firm does work for another organization—such as a local or national government, a university, a hospital, or a large firm, they are owed money. This is called an *account receivable,* which is often shortened to an *AR.*

Since some organizations are not the fastest bill payers in the world, small firms often have to wait 60, 90, or even 120 days for their ARs to be paid. Meanwhile, bills mount up at the small firm.

What can be done to cure this problem? Here's one answer that's good for most small and minority-owned firms:

1. Contact AR lenders—there are many of them around the country.
2. Ask if you can represent the AR lender to small and minority firms. Most lenders are happy to get someone to represent them.
3. Run small classified ads in local papers telling businesses that you have loans available for them. Such an ad might read: Money available for work you've done. For info, call 123-4567.
4. When the small or minority firm calls, ask them for details about the work they've done. They should *not* have yet sent the bill, if you want an AR lender to handle their account.
5. If the AR lender accepts the account, they will quickly advance 80% of the amount owed the small firm. Thus, if your small firm is owed $100,000, the AR firm will pay $0.8 \times \$100,000 = \$80,000$ within 48 hours after getting the information. The balance, $20,000, is paid after the AR firm receives the full payment. Any costs are deducted from the final payment the AR firm gets.

6. Your commission on these deals will vary a little from one AR lender to another. But the AR lender I work with pays a hefty commission on every deal. And this commission continues for the life of the customer. This means that you go on getting commission checks for as long as the small firm deals with the AR lender, even though you might not be part of future deals!

With so many millions of firms seeking loans today, you really can't miss with this business. For more guidance on these types of loans, see the *Small Business Loan Kit* at the back of this book. Getting closer to money will put you on the road to *your* million-dollar fortune!

Other Ways to Use Your RMA

Suppose that you're not turned on by the above ways to make your million-dollar fortune? Are there other ways to use your RMA to make big money? There are plenty. For instance, today you can make big money in:

- Asbestos removal from schools and public buildings
- Acting as a collection agency for businesses
- Converting buildings to condos or co-ops
- Getting 116% financing of garden apartments
- Running an adult (*not* child) day care center
- Conducting aerobic classes and lessons
- Being an airport greeter for people and firms
- Restoring antique autos
- Cleaning apartments and offices
- Publishing how-to books
- Running a child-care referral service
- Organizing people's closets and offices
- Credit counseling for people with credit problems
- Running a computerized videotape dating service
- Analyzing people's dreams for a fee
- Organizing and running garage sales
- Planning and running parties for people and firms
- Hooking up small computers for business networks
- Selling, and installing, facsimile *(FAX)* machines
- Repairing computers in small businesses.

There are—of course—thousands of other businesses you might run and make money from using your RMA. But the above are just a few that might suggest others to you. To show you how you can build your million-dollar fortune from such businesses, let's take a quick look at just a few.

Asbestos Removal

As you've probably heard, asbestos is considered a health hazard. So any building that's insulated with asbestos has to have it removed. Today this is big business because so many buildings use asbestos.

You can make money as a contractor doing the actual work—if you enjoy manual labor. Or you can earn sales commissions selling a contractor to the building owner. The contractor does the work. Or you can make money as a small business loan broker getting AR payments for the contractor. See the earlier coverage of this work in this chapter. But no matter what you do in this field, the money is big because the desire to get the work done is intense!

Acting as a Collection Agency

Today many businesses have problems collecting from their customers. So they often turn their deadbeat clients over to a collection agency to get the money owed them. You can be a collection agency in your area and:

- Earn 50% of the money you collect ($500 on a $1,000 bill you collect)
- Have high prestige among business people in your area
- Learn much about the business you serve.

To become a collection agency is easy. You just set yourself up in business and run small classified ads or send out notices that tell about your services. For more info about getting started, see the *Credits and Collection Kit* described at the back of this book.

Converting Buildings

If real estate is your "thing," then you should look at converting buildings to condos or co-ops. Why? Because when you convert a building you:

- Earn quick money in large chunks, as compared to small monthly rental payments
- Are not tied to one building; you can easily go from one building to another
- Can operate your business in any area of the country where there's a market for condos or co-ops.

In converting buildings, you get control of a suitable property. Then you put the individual apartment units up for sale through a real-estate broker. Or you can sell them yourself if you like this type of work.

The income from the sales will more than pay for the building. Your profit comes from the sales of the units and part of the closing costs. Condos and co-ops are called the Levittown for this generation. Why? Because:

- These types of units are often available at less than a single-family home.
- The closing costs on a co-op are only 3% to 4% of its price; closing costs on a single-family home run 5% to 6% of its price.

And if you can't come up with the cash to buy the building at the start, you can always use a limited partnership. Investors like this approach since they get their money back in a short time—often less than 2 years. And once you package such a deal and sell it off successfully, you'll have investors throwing their money into your face to do more deals. Could there be any easier way to build your million-dollar fortune using your RMA?

Getting 116% Financing of Garden Apartments

There are lenders around who will finance 116% of the cost of garden apartments. Most garden apartments are new, neat, clean, and very nice places to live. So as an owner, you're in a desirable business. To get such financing:

1. Find a suitable garden apartment for sale
2. Do this by checking your local papers and real-estate brokers
3. Work out a suitable price with the seller
4. Contact the lender with info on the property
5. Apply for 116% financing
6. Buy the property
7. Get your mortgaging-out money—see below.

Mortgaging-out money is money you get over and above that needed to buy the property. Let's say that the garden apartment you want to buy costs $5 million. If you can get 116% financing, you receive:

1.16 x $5,000,000	=	$5,800,000
Your cost	=	5,000,000
Mortgage-out $	=	800,000
Closing cost @ 6%	=	300,000 (estimated)
Your net	=	$ 500,000

Now your actual net will probably be less than that shown because you'll have other costs. But this mini-example gets the idea of mortgaging out across. So if you like real estate, consider mortgaging out. It can really put you into the million-dollar fortune class quickly—using your RMA approach!

And remember this—good friend of mine—the money you get at the closing—the $500,000 in this case—is tax-free at that time. Why? Because it's a loan and loans are free of income taxes at the time you receive them.

But when you sell the building and recover the loan amount, a tax will be due, if you sell at a profit. But I'm sure your profit will be high enough to more than pay the taxes!

Be an Airport Greeter for People and Firms

If you travel the world the way I do (my wife and I are steady customers of the Concorde supersonic aircraft), you know how lost you can feel when you arrive in a strange airport. Everyone else—it seems—is embracing friends and relatives. But you're all alone. (Call in your RMA—it will help)!

Airport greeters meet people at an airport, collect their luggage, and get them where they're going. You get a fee for each person you meet. This can range from $25 for "just plain folks" to $500 for VIPs—Very Important People. Your cost? Nothing more than getting to the airport.

How can you let people know you're in the business? Take small space ads in local papers and in the "Yellow Pages" of your phone book.

Publish How-To Books

Everyone in the world today wants to know how to do something. You can satisfy this urge and make big money publishing books on how-to. The book you're reading right now is a how-to book.

As an author of how-to books you get a royalty of about 10% of the list price of the book. Thus, on a $20 book you'll be paid about $2 for each copy sold.

But as publisher of that same how-to book you'll make about $11 per copy! So it's much smarter to be a publisher than an author! How do I know? I'm both. And I can tell you that I make a lot more money as a publisher than as an author. But I still like writing books. That's why I've done some 75 of them!

To get started as a publisher of how-to books, take these easy steps:

1. Decide what field you want to specialize in. Most how-to publishers start in one field and stay in it until they've made a reputation.
2. Once you've picked your field, check to see how many other publishers are in the same field. Don't give up if there are a lot in the field. This means the demand for such books is strong.
3. Decide what your first title will be. If you can write the first book yourself, good! Writing and publishing your own book will teach you a lot about the business.

4. Once you have your first book, get it around as much as you can. Run space ads; get free reviews; get on talk shows. All these steps will help you sell books. And that's why you're in business—to make enough money to make *your* million-dollar fortune!

When you publish how-to books, every day is a new opportunity for you. For instance, a friend of mine publishes how-to books on home care, car repair, and fix-up. Sales weren't the greatest until he received a call from *Parade* magazine saying they would review one of his books in their Sunday issue.

He was ecstatic. With a Sunday circulation of 30 million, he figured he'd sell 3,000 copies of his book—if he was lucky. His real estimate was 2,000 copies.

And—as luck would have it—a monthly magazine with a circulation of 750,000 also agreed to review his book. His estimate of the sales from this review was 750 to 1,000 copies.

So how did his book do? Here are the *Parade* magazine orders and how they arrived:

DATE	NUMBER OF ORDERS
Publication Day (PD)	0
PD + 1	8
PD + 2	25
PD + 3	616
PD + 4	666
PD + 5	395

Each envelope had a check in it, for the book. As of this writing he has gotten 5,400 orders from the excellent *Parade* magazine review. And he's still getting about 30 orders per week from that review!

The monthly magazine results? He received 760 orders—a very nice return. That's about 1 order per 1,000 subscribers.

So you see, publishing how-to books *can* be great fun. And it *can* build your million-dollar fortune. Try it and see for yourself. It did for me!

Help People Solve Their Credit Problems

Today millions of people have some kind of credit problem. You can make money helping them solve such problems. Typical credit problems you'll help cure include:

- Too many inquiries on a person's credit report
- Slow-pay on some bills in the past
- History of bankruptcy
- Record of a judgment against the person
- Incorrect entries on a person's credit report
- Switched credit records between spouses
- Etc.

Some of these problems can be solved just by writing a letter. Others take more work, depending on the type of problem. As a Credit Consultant you can help improve a person's credit history and credit rating.

Why do people want to improve their credit rating? In almost every case the reason is because your client wants to

- Get one or more new credit cards
- Wants to get a loan for some purpose
- Is trying to buy big items (auto, boat, etc.) on credit.

The best way to become a Credit Consultant is to learn all you can about credit, credit ratings, credit cards, etc. You can get books on these subjects or you can take a course such as the one listed at the back of this book. But no matter how you get your info, you'll find it both helpful and interesting. Your own credit will also improve, you'll be pleased to see! So will your RMA.

Get Money from Friendly Sources

Of the thousands of BWBs I meet or talk to every year, almost all have good business ideas. What most need are two things—a better RMA for themselves and some cash to finance their business ideas. I can help you with both these needs. Let's start with the second—*cash*—since we've dealt with your RMA on almost every page of this chapter.

In this world today, there are two types of lenders—friendly and unfriendly. If you can work with the first type you'll have a much nicer deal. My goal is to help you find a friendly lender in *your* area.

Why your area? Because I find that it's somewhat easier to get a loan from people who talk the same way you do. There's less lost motion—you understand each other better!

The friendliest lenders in your area are *development companies.* They may be known by slightly different names in various parts of the country, such as:

- Small business development center
- Minority business center
- Institute for new business ventures
- Division of business expansion
- Product development corporation
- Department of economic development
- Business skills/technical assistance
- Etc.

The main point to keep in mind about these agencies—which are in almost every state—is that they make loans, can provide venture capital, and make *seed money*—startup dollars—available to firms in the state.

So it's worth your while to check out every development company in your state. Why? Because your business ideas are probably great. All you need is some money to put them into action.

As we know from early in this chapter, your RMA helps you *Understand, Act,* and *Obtain.* To use your RMA on development companies, take these steps:

1. You already *Understand* that there are friendly lenders in your area in the form of development companies.
2. You can *Act* by contacting the development companies in your area. To do this, just look in your telephone book under the state listing (often in the blue pages at the back). Call the number given for the development company. Or, if there's no number, call the general information number and ask for the development company number. When you reach the development

company, ask how to apply for a loan, for venture capital, or for seed money—depending on what you seek.

3. Take the needed steps to *Obtain* the funds you need. These steps will vary from one development company to the next. Just do what they say and you'll get the money you seek!

If you can't find "your" development company, I'll be glad to help you, if you're a subscriber to my newsletter. Just call me and I'll give you the name, address, and telephone number of the development company nearest you. I'll also give you the name and title of the person to contact.

And if you need help filling out the papers, I'll be glad to do this—at *no* charge of any kind, if you get my newsletter. Just try me and see!

Your RMA Will Really Work for You

You really *can* build a million-dollar fortune using your Rich Mental Attitude—RMA! I see it every day of the week. Your mind can—and will, if you give it a chance—make *you* rich.

And if you have any trouble getting rich, just use some of my materials. Then—if you have any questions—call me. I may be able to answer that question that's so puzzling. As one reader says:

> I picked up the phone and presto—there you were! I couldn't believe you answer your own phone. Yet you said you did—and you did.
>
> And the answer you gave to my questions were "right on." That's why I'm making money today from the franchise I bought—after you answered my questions. Thanks for all your help!

Remember this: You never know what you can do until you try! That's why your RMA gives you understanding, action, and obtaining what you want. Isn't it about time that you put *your* RMA to work for *your* million-dollar fortune?

DAY 5

Building a million-dollar fortune takes action. This action is fun, rewarding, and full of future promise. Today you start to see how action can take you from a small income to millions. Action helps your mind make you rich. So let's start taking the actions that will build your million-dollar fortune sooner and with less work than you ever thought possible!

CHAPTER 5

TAKE ACTION TO SUCCEED—AND BUILD GREAT WEALTH

ACTION IS YOUR KEY to your million-dollar fortune! It's almost impossible to build wealth without action. If you don't act on your plans you're almost certain to remain poor all of your life. So the way to wealth is through planned action—starting right now!

The Three Keys to Your Million-Dollar Fortune

The three keys to building your million-dollar fortune are all based on action. These keys are:

1. *Action* in your mind. Your mind—as you know by now—can make you rich!
2. *Action* in your goals. You must pick good goals for yourself and then move toward them.
3. *Action* in your doing. Action means that you *do* something to achieve your goals. Like making a phone call, writing a letter, learning new methods.

What you say counts a lot in life. But what you *do* (action) counts a lot more! Once you realize that action gets the results you seek, you'll start taking the steps toward your million-dollar fortune.

You Can't Go Wrong by Taking Action

Some BWBs I meet each year are afraid to start building wealth. Their fear of making a mistake is greater than their fear of being poor forever. When I run into such a BWB—either in person or on the phone—I tell them:

• Thousands of BWBs I've worked with are successful today in many businesses
• Even though they were fearful when they first started in their chosen business
• And none of these BWBs were harmed by taking action in a planned way
• Because their careful plans kept them out of trouble and alerted them to possible problems *before* they happened!

So throw away any fears you may have. If you plan your business as carefully as possible, the chances of going wrong are almost nil. And I'm always here to help you by answering questions or suggesting ways in which you might ensure that your business will be a success.

Plan the Actions You'll Take

To take action you just don't run off and do something! Instead, you plan which actions you'll have to take. Then you go off and act! To plan your actions, take these easy steps:

1. *Decide* what must be done to get your business started. This may mean renting space for a new business or getting the down payment needed to buy a going business. Write down on paper what you figure you must *do* to achieve your starting goal.
2. *Figure* how long each step may take you. Do this by going through each step in your mind and giving it a probable "time needed" number.
3. *Draw* a "time line" that shows how long it will take you to do the things you've listed for your business startup or purchase. If you've never figured times or drawn a

time line before, don't give up! Just make a good guess and jot down the time, as shown in Fig. 5-1.

To help you see what must be done in almost any business, look at Fig. 5-2, which gives you suggested steps. Now don't let these scare you! You don't take every step in every business. Some businesses will need only two or three steps; others may need five or six. But no matter how many are needed, they're fun to take and they *will* make you rich!

Base Your Actions on Your Business Plan

You must—as we said earlier—have a business plan to succeed these days. And your business plan is a beautiful action plan! Why? Because it shows you the steps you must take to make money in the business of your choice.

To see how this might work for you, let's say you're interested in real estate. But your approach is different, as shown in the Executive Summary for your business plan. Here's that Executive Summary for your company, ABC Realty Investments:

ABC Realty Investments will buy single-family homes in an active rental area for all cash, using preapproved loans as the cash source. Prices paid for these homes will be as far below the current market as can be negotiated. Once ownership is obtained, the house will be rented to an acceptable tenant on the basis of offering a one-half ownership in the home. The tenant will pay a higher rent than the going rate but will be offered a share in the tax deductions for interest and real-estate taxes. When the home is sold the tenant will receive one-half the profit, after deducting all sales costs. During the time the tenant is in the home, all normal costs for fuel, electric, water, and maintenance will be paid by the tenant. ABC Realty will have positive cash flow.

Two other paragraphs detail the management and financial data for "your" company. They're not included here since they're unnecessary at this time. Now let's pick the action points from this Executive Summary. They are:

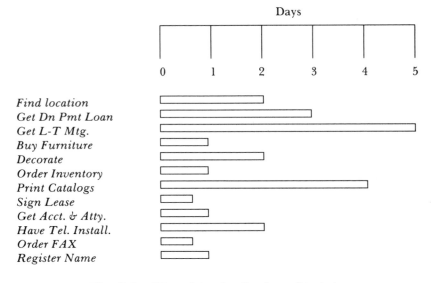

Fig. 5-1   *Time Line for Business Startup.*

Step	Probable Time*	
	By Phone	By Mail
Find location for office or store	3 hr.	2 days
Get loan for down payment on business	2 hr.	3 days
Get long-term mortgage loan for real estate	6 hr.	5 days
Buy office or store furniture	3 hr.	1 day
Have office or store decorated	2 hr.	2 days
Order items to sell to customers	5 hr.	1 day
Get catalogs printed	1 hr.	3 days
Sign lease for office or store	—	1/2 day
Get accountant and attorney	1 hr. each	1 day
Have telephone(s) installed	1 hr.	2 days
Order FAX machine	30 min.	1/2 day
Register business name	—	1 day

* Estimated phone time to call and arrange step listed. Estimated mail time is that needed when using Express Mail both ways.

Fig. 5-2   *Typical Business Startup Steps.*

1. **Look over** the general area you'll invest in to find the "active rental" sections mentioned in your plan. Your action? Look over and find the areas that promise the best rents.
2. **Get preapproved loans** to use to buy the properties you'll invest in. To do this, you'll use your business plan. Your action? Contact real-estate lenders who loan on single-family homes (called SFH in lending lingo).
3. **Find suitable homes** for your investment. You do this by contacting real-estate brokers, watching ads in local papers, and looking for signs saying "For Sale by Owner." Your action? Find suitable investment homes.
4. **Negotiate a suitable price.** The price you pay for your investment house should be 15% to 35% *less* than the going market price. Why? Because this reduces the amount of money you must borrow to buy the house. Your action? Negotiate a price below the going value of the home.
5. **Find a suitable tenant** for the home. Do this by having real-estate brokers look for you, by running ads in local papers, and by contacting large local companies and informing them of the availability of the home. Your action? Get the word around that the house is available.
6. **Figure out what rent to charge** for the house. This should be at least 10% to 20% higher than going rents in your area. Your action? Check local rents and decide what rent you should charge.
7. **Have an attorney draw up** the rental, half-ownership, and payment-of-expenses agreements. Be sure to also get one month's security deposit from the renter to cover any damage. Your action? Get agreements written.
8. **Sell the house** after it has risen enough in price to give you the profit you seek. You can figure an average price increase of 10% a year for well-located, properly maintained SFHs. Your action? Sell the house. Use real-estate brokers, ads in local papers, ads in newspapers published by local firms, and signs on the lawn saying "For Sale by Owner."

You now have eight specific actions to take. And even though we build this company to show you how to take the action steps in your business plan, this *is* a good business for those interested in real estate. Why? For these very simple reasons:

- The price of well-located and property maintained SFH doubles about every 7 years.
- Real estate still offers excellent legal tax shelters that will remain for owners such as you.
- 100% financing is still possible for almost any SFH in a good area.
- Lenders are happy to loan money on well-located SFHs since there are almost no defaults in such loans.
- Having the renter share in the profit from the sale of the property means that it will be well kept at all times. Vandalism will be rare.
- You'll always have a positive cash flow while the property is rented.
- No running costs to you; the renter pays all such costs.
- Monthly profit from the excess of the rent over the mortgage payment is income to you.
- Potential profit from the sale of the property after it has been held for a suitable time is excellent.
- Fast sale for the seller; quick purchase for the buyer. With preapproved loans the buyer does not have to qualify for a loan. The buyer can get into an attractive home for zero cash down.
- Zero cash down allows young families to move into desirable homes while paying only a slight premium in their rent. And they can share in the price rise of the house when it is ready to be sold.
- Few single-family homes are under rent control; so you don't have to fuss with those laws.
- Your organization, as owner of the home, will be entitled to a depreciation deduction on the house. This reduces the income tax that must be paid.

A number of my readers have taken action to start such real-estate empires. And they report great success. Like this one BWB who says:

> Single-family homes will build my fortune much faster than apartment houses. Why? Beause the loans are easier, and faster, to get. Rent control doesn't have any effect on me. Tenants just love well-cared-for homes in good areas of town. And with the price of each home rising as I sleep, I can't go wrong. Meanwhile, I have a steady monthly income without putting in a lot of time. And most of that income

is legally sheltered by the various deductions I'm entitled to take. Thanks for all your books and advice. They've really helped me get started!

You *can* make a fortune in real estate today—if you act! That's the whole key to success in any business. You must:

- Make that needed phone call.
- Send that letter offering results.
- Put that message on the FAX machine.
- Visit the real estate that's for sale.
- Get advice from your attorney and accountant.
- Expand your skills for greater success.

All Action Will Pay You

Many of my BWB readers are in financial trouble. They call me, or visit me, when they're almost at the end of the line. Yet I'm often able to help these BWBs if:

- They're willing to help themselves by taking action to get helpful results
- Even though this action may be painful or may be unpleasant to the BWB
- Using the hope of future financial success as the motivator that produces results.

Some of my BWB readers want to get into real estate as a source of income for themselves. Yet if they have poor credit, they're afraid to even look for (take action, remember) suitable properties. Here's how I help them. We:

1. Show the BWB how to improve his or her credit rating. To do this we have them use one or more of the *Credit Power* books or cassette tapes listed at the back of this book.
2. Help the BWB get a *secured* credit card. This allows the BWB to use a credit card to prove his or her sincerity in paying bills in a timely and complete manner.
3. Teach the BWB, using our various books and kits, the basics of borrowing money for real estate and other business uses. This equips the BWB with the needed info to get the income property he or she seeks.

4. Provide the BWB with an "umbrella" approach to improving his or her financial situation. Such an aproach helps BWBs get control of income property while at the same time they're working at improving their personal credit rating.

But note this, good friend: *All the above steps are based on action!* You cannot—and will not—get the results you seek if you just sit back and wait for the world to come to you.

Build Your Wealth Using a Simple Umbrella

You—we'll say—want to buy a $2-million income property in your area. It will give you a positive cash flow of $5,000 a month, after paying all costs, including loans to take over the property. The seller is seeking a 10% down payment, or $200,000.

I'll assume you have the $200,000, or that you can borrow it. So you have no trouble getting started in real estate.

But suppose a person (not *you*, I'm sure) is in the following condition:

- Poor credit rating because of a slow-pay history
- Bankruptcy three years ago
- Judgment for not paying a disputed bill
- So-so employment history with frequent job changes
- Marital problems of an upsetting kind
- No more than $120 in the bank.

What does such a person do to try to improve his or her life by getting income real estate? Here's an answer that works for thousands of such BWBs:

1. Form a real-estate corporation using the services of a competent attorney. Work out a deal to pay your attorney from the income that the real estate you'll buy will generate.
2. Find suitable real estate to invest in. We'll say (shifting to "you" to save words and space) that the above property is the one you've selected.

3. Work out a deal for the down payment, using your real-estate corporation as the borrower—instead of yourself. By using the corporation (your "umbrella") as the borrower your personal credit history does not come up. Your down payment deal can be a mortgage from the seller (*called a purchase-money mortgage*) for the $200,000. Get this by convincing the seller that you'll work hard to make the property pay you enough income to pay both the seller and the long-term mortgage. If the seller won't agree to such a mortgage, get the down payment reduced as much as possible and then get a loan for what you need. Use your corporation as the borrower.

Once you get your first real-estate property giving you a positive cash flow, you're on your way! Why? Because:

- You'll have a steady income—every month.
- You can use this income to pay both current and past bills.
- Paying these bills will improve your credit rating.
- The building will give you the collateral you need to get the next loan you want to buy your second property. So your "umbrella" is really sheltering any earlier credit problems from the peering eyes of lenders and others who want to check you out.

Again, all these great results are based on action—your action to get the results you seek! Your mind can make you rich—if you act now.

Wealth-Building Actions for Everyone

If real estate is your "bag"—and it is for many BWBs—there are a number of easy wealth-building actions you can take today. If you don't have the down payment for an income property—which *is* the universal problem as I see it today—then consider these actions:

1. Look for tax-sale properties in your local paper. Many such properties are available for zero cash down. You can get useful help from the *Foreclosure Kit* listed at the back of this book.

2. Check with your local banks for repossessed properties they have available. Many of these can be taken over for zero cash down. The bank will even pay the closing costs for you.
3. Seek out sellers who'll give 100% financing of the property they want to sell. You probably won't find these the first time you look. But I can almost guarantee that if you look long enough you'll find a number of sellers who'll give you 100% financing. Readers send me hundreds of letters telling how they got 100% financing for real estate that's giving them a nice monthly income—every month!
4. Find property that's selling for less than its appraised value. Then the long-term mortgage may equal, or exceed, the selling price. When this happens you may be able to walk away with money in your pocket. The book, *How to Finance Real Estate Investments,* by Roger Johnson and the *Real Estate Loan Getters Kit,* both of which are listed at the end of this book, give a number of ways of getting 100% financing for real estate.

The first three methods listed above are best for large cities. The fourth method is good for rural areas.

Simple Actions for Over $100,000 a Year

As some of my readers know, I started my career as a boy of 14 working in the engine room of a merchant ship. I went on to become a licensed officer. Eventually—and reluctantly— I "swallowed the anchor," as we seamen say, and moved into a shoreside job. But the call of the sea is still in my veins. So when a young ex-merchant mariner called me to have lunch, I was happy to meet him. Here's his story:

> On a vacation between trips as Third Engineer on a tanker, Jack was talking to his father-in-law. This gentleman showed him a bill for $199.00 he had just received for having the carpets cleaned in his home. The father-in-law was irate over the size of the bill and the fact that the carpets were not well cleaned.
> "I could do a better job—for less," Jack told him. Looking in the "Yellow Pages" of his phone book, Jack saw about

two full pages of carpet cleaning ads. This didn't discourage him.

Getting on the telephone, Jack started at the letter "A" in his phone book and made calls. "This is ABC Carpet Cleaning; we'll clean any size carpet for $19.99 per room. Would you like me to send you our business card to keep on hand?" In his first 20 calls, Jack got five orders for work!

Using his wife's station wagon, Jack rented some carpet cleaning machines and went to work. Soon he leased a pure white van and had his name painted on the side in sharp black letters.

Today—just 14 months later at this writing—Jack is bringing home a profit of $125,000 a year from his carpet cleaning business. Yet he started without any capital and nothing more than a phone book and a phone! And he has branched out into selling carpet mats. Also, he plans to franchise his business soon. This could bring him up to $5 million in franchise fees over a few years.

"I wanted to go into real estate. But it seemed to take a long time. This way I'm in real estate but the money comes in a lot faster," Jack told me. "And I'm not out to sea away from my family. I'm home every night!"

Jack took a number of very simple *actions* to go from spending six months a year at sea to being a free, independent businessperson. These simple actions?

1. Picking up a telephone and making some calls
2. Doing the work being paid for in the best way he could
3. Giving an impression of cleanliness and efficiency
4. Planning to branch out in the same line of business

Now I know that carpet cleaning in real estate may not be your bag. But this true story does show that:

1. You can get started—simply and easily.
2. You do *not* need a lot of capital to get started.
3. Having a clear concept of your goals will pay off.

As an aside, I asked Jack if he ever missed the sea—as I often do. He looked at me and replied: "Yes, Ty, I do. Every now and then I think about it. Especially when I see my classmates from the school ship who are now Chief Engineers and Skippers. But I'd rather have my own business than be stranded out on some ship for months at a time!"

You—I firmly believe—can take simple actions that will bring in more than $100,000 a year—quickly and easily. It's just a matter of taking actions, as Jack did. You simply pick the field you like and start taking those crucial steps to *your* success.

Where to Find Millions for Any Business

Sometimes there's so much money around that people stumble over it without even knowing it is! For instance a reader in the Midwest called to say:

> "I need a 90% loan on a home. I've tried almost all the lenders in your *Comprehensive Loan Sources* book but none will go beyond 80%. What can I do?" My answer? "Keep trying other lenders in the book. Try some S&Ls—they like homes." Reading the reaction of this great reader through the telephone line, I could tell he wasn't too happy with my response. Yet he called back an hour later saying, "Thanks for kicking me. I got a 90% lender out of your book! It was the next one I called." Then he gave the name of the lender. "I'm sorry I had to 'kick' you so hard," I said. "But pushing on often works magic. It did with you!"

The millions you can get for any business (and real estate *is* a business, remember) can come from business development companies. Almost every state has a business development company (the *friendly* lender of Chapter 4) that provides:

- Seed, or startup, capital
- Free business advice of many types
- Long-term loans for worthwhile business purposes
- Venture capital for new businesses
- Site location
- Minority business assistance
- Import-export
- Problem solving
- Market information
- Hiring incentives/employee training
- Grants—up to $500,000 from some states.

Many of these business development companies are funded by both the state and local firms. Some even have federal funds. But all can be important to you in getting money for real estate or business use. A recent loan of $4 million we obtained for an import-export company startup came through a business development company.

How can *you* contact such a company in your state? That's easy. You just take some simple actions. They are:

1. Look up—in your phone book—the name and phone number of *your* business development company. You'll find them in the state pages. Or, if you're a one-year, or longer, subscriber to my monthly newsletter, *International Wealth Success,* you can call me and I'll give you the name and phone number of the business development company in your state.

2. Call your business development company. Tell the person answering what you're looking for. You will probably be advised to call another number in the group for the specific help you need. (The BWB who got the $4-million loan had to call three numbers. But he *did* get his loan! This is the only measure I use—results.)

3. Do—act—what you're told to do to get your loan. The BWB mentioned above needed letters of recommendation. He asked me to write one on my company letterhead— which I did. You may be asked the same—or something else. The whole key is to *do*—act—what you're asked to do. Without the needed action, millions may slip through your hands!

4. Get the money you need. The whole key to this approach is to get the money you need for your real-estate or business deal. Once you have the money, be certain to take the steps needed to start building your wealth.

I'm so certain that you can build wealth once you have the money that I offer loans to readers of my newsletter. Any two-year subscriber can apply for a business or real-estate loan repayable in any way chosen. The loans run from one day (yes, we have made a few one-day loans) to seven years. Our interest rate is low. But not as low as it used to be. Therein lies a story which I must tell you—right here.

For years we offered—and made—business and real-estate loans at 6% simple interest. The term *simple interest* means that you pay interest *only* on the money you have in your hand. That is, your interest cost goes *down* every time you make a loan payment. Further, these loans were made:

- With *no* points, fees, retainers, or any charges of any other kind—and certainly *NO* front money!
- To BWBs throughout the world, regardless of race, color, creed, etc.
- For active real estate or business purposes.

When some people heard about our 6% loans—which we made regularly—they said: "That's impossible. It can't be!" Or "Why would anyone make loans at 6% when they can get 8% on a CD? It's fishy."

Good friend, there are plenty of states in this great country of ours that make 3% loans, 4% loans. There are even some that make *NO INTEREST LOANS!* Yet the idiot comment-ators on our 6% loans couldn't shut up.

After a few such reactions over a period of two years, I said: "Fine; we'll double the rate to 12%. Then the idiots will believe." Since then we haven't had a single such comment as "It's impossible!" The idiots are happy to pay twice as much because it fits in with their limited experience.

The lesson here? Never offer too good a deal. People won't believe you because they want to make things harder for themselves! This way they suffer more and seem to enjoy it. P.S. We *still* do offer 6% loans for real-estate and business emergencies. So far no one has found fault with this approach!

Mine the Home Equity Gold Rush

Today banks and mortgage lenders are hungering to make home equity loans. These are loans on the ownership portion a home owner has in his or her home. For example, let's take a typical suburban home today:

Market value	$300,000
Amount owed on mortgage	100,000

Equity   200,000
Amount you can borrow = 75% of equity,
or 0.75 × $200,000 = $150,000

The amount you can borrow is put into a line of credit. This means you do *not* pay interest on the money available to you ($150,000 in this case) until you take some of it. Then you pay only on the amount you take. For example:

Line of credit = $150,000
Amount used =   30,000
Interest payable only on $30,000—not $150,000

Why do I suggest using the home equity loan? For a number of very good reasons. These are:

1. When you go to use a "product" lenders are pushing, they welcome you into the "fold."
2. Lending officers have quotas to get a certain number of "hot" loans made (the one they're pushing). So the loan officer doesn't fight you—he or she almost pulls you to the desk to get you to start filling out papers. Or, if you want to deal by mail or phone, you're welcome to work that way.
3. Your whole experience is friendly, happy, productive. You get the money you seek without a lot of hassle.

How can you get a home equity loan? There are a number of ways, all of which are being used by my readers every day. These ways are:

1. Use the equity in your own home, if you own one. This is the fastest, and surest, way to get the money you seek. Your action? Apply for the loan!
2. Use the equity in a friend's home. Pay your friend a fee for using the equity. Your action? Find a friend who's willing to work with you.
3. Use the equity in a relative's home. Pay a fee, even if the relative refuses. Why? Because this keeps the deal on a business basis—which it should be. Your action? Find a relative who will work with you to get the loan you seek.
4. Get a business partner or associate to allow you to use his or her home equity. Again, pay a fee for this service.

Your action? Find a suitable business partner who can offer equity in a home as collateral for the loan you need.

Now don't let your natural resistance to borrowing get in your way. Many people resist borrowing because they somehow think it's "bad." Borrowing is *never* bad when you're planning to use the borrowed money to make money!

When you borrow to buy something for your personal pleasure you must be very careful—especially if the item goes down in value as time passes. Sure, you *do* get pleasure from your purchase—and that's important in life. But the item does not earn income for you. This is why some people have the "bad" image of borrowing. (To borrow money by mail, see Exhibit 5-1).

How to Get Rich in MAIL ORDER CA$H LOAN DOLLARS.

°Overcome BAD CREDIT for yourself and others!

°Get CASH in a flash--maybe one day, or less!

°Find an "Angel" for your cash needs!

°Develop signature-loan MONEY POWER!

°Rate YOUR loan chances in minutes!

°Wipe out ALL DEBTS with just one loan!

°Deal by mail--NO interviews; NO pain!

°Get liquid assets for any personal need!

°Get INTEREST-ONLY mail-order loans!

°Be the "fastest loan broker" around!

°Get DOZENS of different kinds of loans!

°Be a MAIL-ORDER UNSECURED SIGNATURE LOAN wheeler-dealer!

°Make friends with money lenders forever!

°Get MAIL-ORDER LOAN convenience, speed, efficiency, confidentialty!

°Earn BIG FEES helping others get quick unsecured signature loans!

°Know who's lending for what use!

°Laugh "all the way to the bank" NOW!

°Deal by mail and avoid face-to-face hassles and arguments!

GET UNSECURED PERSONAL SIGNATURE LOANS FOR YOUR CLIENTS OR YOURSELF using the IWS MAIL-ORDER LOAN SUCCESS SYSTEM--the fastest way to get a signature loan today! Learn how to deal with lenders--prepare winning loan applications--help yourself or others to the BILLIONS available for unsecured loans! Build your own, or your client's loan rating fast! It's ALL here--plus much, much more in this NEW powerful SYSTEM!

Written by Ty Hicks, a man who has supervised the lending of some $50-million in all types of unsecured signature loans, this SYSTEM is just what's needed to get people the money they seek! And YOU can use the SYSTEM for your clients, or for yourself. It works, works, works for YOU! And it works for anyone you're helping get a loan. The SYSTEM gives you thousands of lenders to contact--shows YOU how to build your own list of willing and interested lenders! Send your check or money order for your SYSTEM today! Get loans SOON!

THIS IS THE ORDER BLANK

$$$ $$$$$$

$ Here's $100. Send me my MAIL-ORDER LOAN SUCCESS SYSTEM. If you wish, you can call Ty $
$ Hicks with your credit-card (Master or Visa) order at 516-766-5850 9am to 10 pm. Have $
$ your credit card ready? Ask Ty any questions you may have! $

$ NAME _____ Apt/Suite #_____ $

$ ADDRESS _____ CITY_____ STATE_____ ZIP_____ $

$ Send check or money order to: IWS, Inc., 24 Canterbury Rd, Rockville Centre NY 11570 $

Exhibit 5-1

Borrowing money to make money is *never* bad. As long as you take action to make the borrowed money earn for you more than it costs you, your future wealth is almost certain! Using borrowed money to earn money is one of the smartest methods to build riches ever discovered. Since I'm certain your ideas for building wealth are good, all you need is the money to get started. Good ideas combined with action win—every time!

Other Ways to Get Money Through Action

If the home equity loan doesn't appeal to you, don't give up. There are plenty of other ways to get the money you seek for your business. These ways include:

1. *Grants* from corporations, foundations, or governments. A grant never has to be repaid, if you do the work for which the grant was made. Today grants are being made for both profit-making and nonprofit organizations. You *must* take specific steps to get a grant. But your action can pay off in interest-free money that never needs to be repaid.

2. *Private money* comes from wealthy people who want to see their funds grow when invested in a worthwhile business. The money you get may be in the form of a loan or in equity—where the person buys a portion of your business. When private money is in the form of a loan, it must be repaid over a period of time—usually three to five years. In the form of equity, private money never need be repaid. But you do own less than 100% of your company. And any profits must be shared with your money source. So it does cost you to have equity money.

3. *Private placements* of stock or participations in your company can get you millions of dollars. And recent revisions of the rules for Regulation D by the Securities and Exchange Commission (SEC) make it much easier to raise the money you need. Today you can sell your securities to an unlimited number of accredited investors, and to 35, or fewer, nonaccredited investors. Today, an accredited individual invester has an income of $200,000;

couples a joint income of $300,000. Other accredited investors are thrift institutions, broker-dealers, corporations, partnerships, and business trusts with assets of more than $5 million. In today's world, these requirements are easy to meet.

4. *Federal government loans* can be obtained today with much less paperwork than in the past. And these loans, especially those from the Small Business Administration (direct loans or guarantees), are made much faster. Since money is money—no matter what its legitimate source— you should take action to check *every* possible way of getting the money you seek. With any government loan, you'll have to fill out some papers. While this may seem a chore, it really helps you see your business as others do. This is valuable to you because you get a clearer picture of what you're trying to do.

There are dozens of other dependable sources of money for you. They're mentioned in various chapters in this book. Take action to see which ones will work with you. You'll never know unless you do. So:

1. *Make* that needed telephone call.
2. *Write* that letter asking for help.
3. **Ask** a friend, relative, or business associate to be of use to you in getting money.
4. *Look up* information on the sources that might help you.

Action Does Get and Make Money

When you decide to act, your mind becomes goal-oriented and directed. This gets your whole body ready to find, and earn, money. Your entire mental set brings you to the point where your mind can make you rich!

That's why I keep urging you to take action toward your future wealth. You *will* get rich if you direct your mind to the sources of wealth that are all about you today. And if you have problems along the way, just remember that I am ready to help you through my newsletter and many other books.

What's more—you can get me by phone or mail. Or, if

you want to visit in person, just let me know. I'll be glad to meet you in my office at a time that's convenient to you.

I say all of this assuming that you *will* act when the time is right. And there never was a better time than right now. Thousands of my readers prove this every year. You could be the next to write me about your fortune and how you're working toward it, as this reader did

> After having bought and used your *Money Raisers Directory of Bank Credit Card Programs,* I have to admit that the price was the best twenty bucks (really $19.95) that I have spent in years.
>
> Not only have I been able to obtain additional cards, but I have been able to "clean up" my credit profile of erroneous and inaccurate information, and still maintain a good rapport with the several credit reporting agencies.
>
> Anytime that I get a chance to recommend your credit card program, I shall be glad to do so.

That's the story—*action to get results!* When will *you* start to take action to get the wealth results you seek? There never was a better time for you than right *now*!

DAY 6

People—like your mind—can make you rich! By winning people to your cause, you get help that can build your riches faster than you think. Today we take charge of our future by seeing the many ways people can help us reach our goals in life. At the same time we'll expand our world to include new ideas and new ways to get rich.

CHAPTER 6

WIN PEOPLE TO YOUR CAUSE—AND GET ANY NEEDED HELP

No MATTER WHAT BUSINESS you pick to earn your million-dollar fortune, you'll be dealing with people. You just can't avoid it! These people might be your:

- Customers—thank goodness for them!
- Suppliers—you'll almost always need some supplies.
- Employees—you can't do everything yourself!
- Regulators—some branch of some government is almost certain to be interested in your business.
- Trade association—it can be a great source of help and reliable information for your business.
- General business groups—there are many of them and they can help you earn *your* fortune.
- Benefit groups—insurance companies, pension funds, etc. can help you build a secure future with your business.

Now I know you may be a loner. Millions of BWBs are. But you really can't do everything yourself! If you try to, you're almost certain to limit your earnings. Thus, this year I conducted a survey among my newsletter readers to find out the largest amount earned in a one-person business. Here are the findings:

- Half the one-person businesses earned $250,000 a year, or less.
- Most one-person businesses earned between $200,000 and $250,000.

- The highest earning business earned $435,000 but this person had the help of a part-time secretary.

So if you want to earn a million-dollar fortune, you'll have to deal with people. And the actions you take with them will control your maximum earnings. Let's see how you can act to win people to your cause and earn your millions. We'll look at each of the major classes of people you'll work with.

Thank Goodness for Customers

Customers make your business! You may never see a customer, may never talk to one. But without customers your business will not exist. So we say thank goodness for customers.

To serve your customer well, take a pencil and piece of paper and put at the top: What My Customers Want. Then list your customers' wants as they come into your mind. Don't try to decide which want is more important than others. Just list the wants at random.

Doing this will teach you a lot about your business. Why? Because it will show you:

- What's important to your customers
- Which way to change your services or products
- Where your greatest chances for high earnings are
- What items will sell best for you.

I did this for my business—which is publishing financial, real-estate, mail-order, and import-export books, kits, and other helpful information. The random list I came up with is shown in Fig. 6-1.

After the list was written down, I went back over it and numbered the items from 1 on. Number 1 was the most important item to my readers, in my view. Number 2 was second in importance, etc. The revised list is shown in Fig. 6-2.

WHAT MY CUSTOMERS WANT

Loans for business or real estate
Help in finding certain products or services
Personal loans for themselves or relatives
Advice on where to get business grants
Answers to questions about specific businesses
Where to find cosigners for loans
Names/addresses of state organizations helping business
Information on import-export and how to get started in it
Best ways to promote by mail order and direct mail
What results to expect from advertising of various types
How can I get real estate for zero cash down
Fast delivery of needed products
Ability to pay bills by credit card
Personal meeting with Ty Hicks.

Fig. 6-1   *Customer Wants List Jotted Down at Random.*

CUSTOMER WANTS LIST CATEGORIZED
(1 is strongest demand)

1. Loans for business or real estate
2. Personal loans for themselves or real estate
3. Where to find cosigners for loans
4. Advice on where to get grants for business
5. Answers to questions about specific businesses
6. Help in finding certain products or services
7. Names/addresses of state organizations helping business
8. Information on import-export and how to get started in it
9. How can I get real estate for zero cash down
10. Best ways to promote by mail order and direct mail
11. What results to expect from advertising of various types
12. Fast delivery of needed products
13. Ability to pay bills by credit card
14. Personal meeting with Ty Hicks

Fig. 6-2   *Customer Wants List Categorized by Degree of Importance. A rating of 1 is the most important; 14, the least important.*

Based on Fig. 6-2, here's what I did for my customers to serve them better:

- Started a loan department to lend money to BWBs wanting to start or buy a business of their own
- Made available "hot" lists of lenders of many types for business, real estate, import-export, etc.
- Opened my telephone consulting service using a toll-free number so readers can get free advice, order books, or kits directly—day or night
- Accepted credit-card orders for all items to speed the service and products to every customer
- Use Express Mail and the various courier services to deliver books and kits overnight in the U.S., and in just days anywhere in the world
- Take FAX orders, loan applications, and other documents in just hours—again to speed service to readers.

This business made my million-dollar fortune quickly—and with lots of fun. The results clearly showed me anyone can do the same. That's why I urge every reader who has customers (and who doesn't) to get pencil and paper and list what these customers want.

Knowing what your customers will want can help you tailor a new business to their exact needs. Think of the businesses you see almost every day and how they cater to their customer wants. Thus:

- *Fast-food businesses:* Quick service; roadside service; moderate prices; disposable containers; popular menus
- *Personal computers:* Programs needed by small business (accounting, inventory, billing, etc.), games for young users; exam reviews for students
- *Auto repair:* Specialists in rapid-wear items—such as exhaust systems, brakes, shocks, etc. Fast service; convenient locations; long guarantees; attractive waiting areas.

Give your customer what he or she wants and you'll prosper. Neglect your customer and your business will decline.

Go the Extra Mile for Every Customer

Nearly every business makes a mistake now and then. In our business we get thousands of orders through the mail, over the phone, by FAX, etc. While our people are sincere and really try, a mistake happens now and then.

I insist that the mistake be corrected immediately. If possible, we call the customer on the phone. (When a customer has an unlisted phone number, you can't call them). So you must write. Here's the way we handle errors:

- Calling (if possible), or writing the customer as soon as the error is discovered, we say:
- "We're very sorry—we goofed! It's our fault. The correct item is being sent to you today via the fastest way possible. And, in appreciation of your patience with us, you can order any IWS book or kit costing $25, or less, and we'll send it to you *free* of charge. Again—we're very sorry we made this mistake."

What does such an approach to your loyal (and suffering, in this case) customer do? It:

- Gets the customer the *correct* item ordered—which, after all—good friend—is what the customer really wants from you!
- Shows the customer that your're big enough to admit, and correct, an error you made. (It takes a big person to admit a fault.)
- Convinces the customer you're sincere when you offer a free product as a show of appreciation.

Going the extra mile with *every* customer builds loyalty. Some of my customers have been with me for more than 20 years. I feel they're part of my extended family. There's nothing I wouldn't do for them.

You, too, can—and in my opinion, should—go the extra mile with every customer. Here are simple—and easy—steps you can take:

1. Pay attention to every customer. Neglecting any customer can only lead to problems.
2. Stay in touch with customers. Answer their letters when

they write. Talk to them when they call you on the telephone.

3. Keep your promises! If you promise to call back in an hour, do so. Don't forget any customer—ever!

4. Admit errors; correct them instantly. Don't try to squirm out of your duty. Do what must be done—now!

5. Never be afraid of a customer. Tell the person what the situation is. Level with every customer and they'll come back to spend more money with you!

6. Don't "play office" with customers. Be ready to talk to every customer as soon as you can. Face up to any complaints and settle them quickly.

7. Never underprice your services or products! Some people who buy a $15 book from me want $150 in consulting services free. I tell them I'll be glad to help. But my time is priced at $250 an hour, unless they're subscribers to my newsletter. Then my time is free to them.

Going the extra mile with every customer will put millions into your pocket. So doesn't this approach really make sense? It does to me.

Our biggest help to customers is the loans we offer for active business and real-estate purposes. These loans have helped many BWBs get started in a successful business. Offered to two-year subscribers to our newsletter, *International Wealth success,* the loans are our most important "extra mile" for our customers. Info on these loans is given earlier in this book, in Chapter 5.

Be Nice to Your Suppliers—It Pays

You're almost certain to have to buy supplies for your business. Surely, you'll need a pen or two, some stamps, paper, etc. The people who sell you these items are your suppliers.

Why should you be nice to *all* suppliers? For a number of very good reasons. Like:

• Possibility of lower prices for supplies
• Useful trade info that will be passed on to you
• Good credit references if you pay your bills on time
• Sources of credit when you need it

- Help with professional references to accountants, attorneys, etc.

If you're in the mail-order/direct-mail/bookstore business, the way I am, you'll deal with several types of suppliers, such as:

- Printers and binders
- United States Postal Service
- Overnight couriers
- Office equipment firms
- Office supply firms
- Telephone company.

Pay your bills on time, and suppliers such as these will give you good service—year-round. Neglect paying on time and you'll have real problems. With some suppliers, of course, it's cash on the barrelhead. So be sure to plan ahead for such cash expenses.

Keep in close touch with your suppliers. Visit them. If you can't, call on the phone. Or write a friendly letter. And:

- Write a short thank-you note when paying your bill.
- Remember anniversaries with a note—such as the first full year of business, the fifth year, etc.
- Praise their work to others in front of them.
- Recommend other customers to them.

Suppliers can help you—too! For example, if you need a cosigner for a business loan, a supplier may be your answer. Thus, one reader recently told me:

> I needed a $50,000 loan for my business. But my credit was shaky and the banks wouldn't talk to me. I scratched around looking for a cosigner because one of the banks I contacted told me that's what I'd need to get a loan from them. But none of my relatives, friends, or business associates was willing to cosign for me. One day I mentioned this to my paint supplier (I'm a painting contractor). He asked me a few questions about the loan and then said: "I'll be glad to cosign for you if you'll go on buying paint from me." That's all I needed. I got the loan and it's almost repaid in full—way ahead of time! And I'm buying more paint than ever from my friendly supplier.

You can even save money by being nice to suppliers. For instance, you can get lower prices by:

- Paying cash with order—often 10% to 15% off
- Signing a long-term contract for your supplies
- Dealing with discount suppliers—there are many around today.

In a small business you *must* control every cost. Being nice to suppliers is one way to control—and reduce—costs. So start being nice today! It makes the world a better place and can put money into your deep pockets.

Build Employee Loyalty Every Day

As your business grows, you'll soon learn you can't do everything yourself. So you'll start looking for help. Good employees—whether permanent or temporary—can make you rich! So try to build employee loyalty every day of the week. You'll never regret this step.

To build employee loyalty, take these easy steps:

- Pay fair wages—a little more than your competition pays.
- Allow employees to make decisions about their jobs.
- Praise each employee at least once a week.
- Make everyone feel important to your firm's success.

In our business we employ both young and not-so-young people. And we often find that the not-so-young people are more dependable than the younger ones. Now I'm not knocking the young. It's just that they seem to have more problems in their personal lives, which take them away from their job.

Our eldest worker is—at this writing—84. Yet he works round-the-clock getting the job done. He even "bugs" me to do this, do that. I tell him I'm the boss. But he still says "Do this; do that!" And do you know what? I do it!

There are other important reasons why good employees are important to you. For example, good help:

- Allows you to get away from the business now and then without worrying about the "place blowing up"

- Allows you to spend time on planning, on getting new customers, on developing future income sources
- Allows you to make money on the efforts of others. And this—good friend—is the real key to great wealth, to that million-dollar fortune! Making money on the efforts of others expands *your* earning capacity far beyond your wildest dreams.
- Allows you to take a vacation—to re-create. Without an occasional vacation you'll go stale in your business. Sure, you may lose a few dollars while you're gone because no one can sell as well as you do. But my experience shows that people will almost always come back and order later. So you really don't lose that much income!

Good employees can give you new ideas about your business. They may even have some ideas that are better than yours! While I hate to admit it, some of my employees have come up with some of my most profitable ideas. And I really thank them (and reward them) for these great ideas!

Treat Regulators with Respect

Every business has at least one regulator looking at it. Most have several regulators to serve, such as:

- The Internal Revenue Service
- The U.S. Department of Labor
- The United States Postal Service
- Your state income tax department or bureau
- Your state labor department
- The Better Business Bureau
- The Federal Trade Commission
- Consumer Service Department
- Securities Exchange Commission.

Now don't let this list scare you. Almost *no* small business has to deal with all these regulators. And even if you did, it would be easy if you follow my proven—and tested—ways of working with them. To deal successfully and profitably with any regulator, take these easy steps:

1. ***Recognize*** that every regulator can be very powerful in the life of your business. Failure to recognize this can lead to many unneeded problems.
2. ***Be polite at all times to every regulator!*** If you try to pick a fight with a regulator, you'll get one. And I suggest to you—good friend—that it's *not* wise to ever pick a fight with any regulator! You can regret it for years, after the regulator uses his or her power to correct your ways.
3. ***Use the regulator's title*** when addressing him or her. Thus, if the regulator has the title of Inspector, address the regulator at all times as Inspector _____
   This is most important. Why? Because regulators place great emphasis on their titles. And they want you to recognize and respect their title at every chance you have. Further, if you do not use the title in parts of your conversation, then revert to the conventional "Yes, Sir," or "Yes, M'am." Why? Because regulators expect respect!
4. ***Never try to make a regulator uncomfortable.*** We've all heard stories of trying to make a regulator uncomfortable in an office or factory so he/she will leave sooner. This just doesn't work. What does work—from my experience—is to be polite, helpful, and considerate of the regulator at all times. Provide the usual business facilities—desk, telephone, light, heat, etc.—to the regulator. Then leave him or her alone to do the work for which the visit was made.
5. ***Never offer a regulator a bribe.*** You'll only wind up in trouble and the regulator won't have any sympathy for you. Bribes never get the results you seek. So cross the thought of a bribe off—right now!
6. ***Be prepared for the regulator's visit.*** If you need papers of any kind for the regulator to review, have them ready— neatly arranged. Never try the "shoebox trick" of passing a large box of receipts to a regulator and saying: "Here, you want a receipt, find it for yourself." You won't get respect from the regulator with this tactic. Instead, have your receipts neatly arranged by month or year. When asked for a specific receipt, take it from your file and hand it to the regulator. Come up with the requested receipt a few times and you'll find the regulator convinced that you're honest, reliable, and dependable.
7. ***Speak when spoken to—never volunteer any information*** to a regulator. The more you say, the more you may

have to provide to answer a simple question. Where legal problems might arise in an interview with a regulator, you should have your attorney at your side. Likewise, with tax and accounting reviews by regulators, you must have your accountant present, unless it's a simple task of providing a receipt or other simple evidence.

Where you're in a business that has many potential regulator reviews, prepare a business profile to give to regulators. I did this for my business many years ago and it really helps. The items my business profile covers—and which you should consider for yours—are:

- Date founded
- Date incorporated
- Names of principals
- Career data of principals
- Attorney's name/address
- Date of joining each organization of which firm is a member
- Classified listing of the firm's customers—in our case this is bookstores, libraries, universities, government offices, etc.
- Place founded
- State of incorporation
- Addresses of principals
- Accountant's name/address
- Names of organizations of which the firm is a member
- Principal products of the firm
- Our banking connections.

With this profile at the ready, I just hand it to a regulator when asked "What does your company do?" Since we have some of the top organizations in the world—such as the U.S. government, Harvard University, major banks, etc.—as our customers, our credibility is immediately established in the regulator's mind. Of course, questions can still be asked, But we have established who we are, what we do, and who our customers are. That really helps.

Over the years I've been visited by many regulators. In all these interviews, I've never had a fight. Nor have I been penalized for my business practices. While each interview made me a little nervous, let me say that I always:

- Learned good business practices from each regulator
- Got a better picture of what they were seeking from business
- Saw that each regulator is human, and understanding

- Found that regulators have their pressuress, too, like everyone else in business.

So look upon the visit of a regulator as a learning experience. The regulator is just one of the many people who can help your business grow. And every regulator can help you toward your million-dollar fortune! Your mind can make you rich, but you'll usually need some help. See Exhibit 6-1 for good rules on dealing with any regulator—anywhere!

GOOD RULES FOR DEALING WITH ANY REGULATOR

1. Answer every letter from a regulator *instantly*. Do *not* put the regulator's letter aside to "work on later." Answer it *now!*
2. Return a regulator's phone call *instantly*. If the regulator is not available when you call, state exactly who you are, what company you're with, and why you're calling— to return the regulator's call. Be sure the person answering gets everything you say written down correctly.
3. Use Certified Mail, Return Receipt Requested, when writing any regulator. Then you have proof of mailing and receipt. Include, below the date on your letter, the notation: Via Certified U.S. Mail, No. _____, Return Receipt Requested. Insert the Certified Mail sticker number in the space shown. Then you have court-acceptable proof that you *did* answer the regulator's letter.
4. Don't be afraid to call the regulator to clarify any points in the regulator's letter or phone call. *Remember:* A regulator can put you out of business, attach your firm's bank account, or take your assets (home, auto, machines, etc.) away from you. So get any misunderstood points cleared up immediately.
5. Contact your accountant and attorney as soon as you hear from any regulator. Ask what steps you should take. Then follow the advice of your professional advisor.
6. Provide the regulator with just the information requested—nothing more. Don't volunteer any information beyond that requested.
7. Remember at all times that dealing with a regulator is very serious business. Be polite, cooperative, and prompt. And don't forget to say a sincere prayer for good guidance!

Exhibit 6-1

Get Help from Trade Associations

There are thousands of trade associations in the world today. And one or more are almost certain to be of help to you. Further, trade association dues are generally low. So it won't break you to join one.

What's in it for you when you join a trade association? Lots. You can expect:

- Information on your business—such as typical costs, profits, employee earnings, etc.
- Data on how to overcome business problems; info on how other people in the same business as you are growing and prospering
- Meetings with others in the same business at which you can share info, swap stories of successes, etc.
- "Mental support" to help you overcome problems that may have you down.

Our firm belongs to two trade associations. The annual dues for the two totals less than $500 a year. Yet we get thousands of dollars on info from each association. And they're always there to answer any questions we may have. You can expect the same in your business!

Don't Overlook General Business Groups

The best general business group you and your firm can join is—in my opinion—the Better Business Bureau. Why? For these reasons. Being a member of the BBB tells people that:

- You and your business support ethical dealing in all business matters.
- Your firm has provided background info to the BBB to establish your dependability and honesty.
- You will submit to arbitration in the event of a dispute between yourself and a customer.
- Any prospective customer can check you out at the BBB and learn if there are any complaints on file against you.

Being a BBB member helps build your credibility with

prospective customers. It also lets the community know that you're not in the business of ripping anyone off.

There are a number of other general business organizations you might want to join. They do many things, such as:

- Representing small businesses in Washington, D.C.
- Offering hospitalization plans
- Getting discounts on business purchases
- Publishing directories of various types.

I'll leave it up to you to decide if you want to join any such group. My experience shows that being a member of one such group can help you and your business. And the cost is never excessive!

Get Extra Benefits from Your Business

There are many benefits from having your own business. Among these are benefit plans for you which your company pays—at *no* cost to you. Like:

- A pension for you when you retire
- Life insurance on your life
- Hospitalization and medical plans of various types
- Unemployment insurance for you

These benefit plans can be simple—or deluxe. The whole key is the amount your business can pay. And since most benefit plans are tax-deductible to the company and nontaxable to you (until retirement for pensions), you might as well take as many advantages as you can. It will help you make *your* million-dollar fortune sooner.

Many small firms also use a profit-sharing plan with the money put away tax-free until the person retires. When invested wisely—such as by a large insurance company—your profit-sharing money can grow while you sleep. And meanwhile, your company benefits from a lower tax rate! You really can't beat the many advantages offered you by your own business.

To start any of these plans, be sure to consult a competent professional. Advice from such a person is free. And you can learn a great deal from such people in a short time. So go and lock in the benefits to which you're legally entitled— right now.

Get Started for Pennies

"All of this sounds great," you say. "But I don't have a business yet. So how can I win people to my cause?" That's a good question. Especially if you don't have tons of money to start, or buy, a business. But don't give up. You *can* get started for pennies. Here's how—in a business *you* might love:

1. Recognize—here and now—that if you can sell by mail you can get started for just pennies. And it *can* be done!
2. Ask yourself if you think you'd be happy in the *international mail-order business*. In such a business you deal only by mail and rarely talk to a customer or even see what you're selling! And you can get started for just pennies.
3. Think about what kinds of items you'd like to export. You have the whole world open to you. Exporting is easier than you think and it can bring you quick riches. But you must be happy with what you're exporting. Why? Because you'll do a better job and this shows through. Your overseas customers will keep reordering from you. So your business becomes almost an automatic money machine, building your riches day by day. But you *must* think about what items you want to handle to make your million-dollar fortune. *Remember:* Your mind can make you rich!
4. Knowing what you want to export, find overseas firms seeking such items. Do this by getting leads from the *Import-Export Kit* described at the back of this book, from airlines serving overseas countries, from steamship companies delivering overseas, or from governments— both domestic and foreign—that seek to encourage trade.
5. Once you find an overseas firm seeking an item you want to export, look for a domestic firm or firms supplying

it. Contact the firm by mail or phone (for pennies) and ask if they have the item you're seeking to export. If they do, try to get some price quotes. These can either be given in the form of a Price Sheet, or by phone or mail.

6. Write the overseas firm (use surface mail if you want to save money) and tell the company that you can supply the item they want. Now if you're seeking speed, you can use a Telex service to contact the overseas firm or today you can use a FAX machine. You needn't buy either type machine at the start. Instead, you can use a service that will charge you a nominal price.

7. If the overseas firm asks for a quote, give it to them, adding a suitable amount—usually 10% of the total price, for your commission. (This 10% commission can be adjusted upward or downward, depending on competition, the amount of the order, etc. The details are covered in the *Import-Export Kit* mentioned earlier.)

8. When your quote is accepted, contact the supply firm with details of the order. Get them to ship it for you. Or contact a custom-house broker (see your "Yellow Pages") and have that firm handle the work for you.

9. Collect your fee and go on to the next export job. All for just pennies.

Many of my readers hit the big money in export on their first try. Others take a little longer. *Remember:* Exporting is really an international mail-order business. But there are a number of differences between the consumer mail-order business (such as selling gadgets, clothing, food, etc.) and the international mail-order business. These important differences are:

- The overseas firm is buying to resell to make money. So you don't have problems with a change of mind, or a dislike for a certain color, etc.
- Overseas firms pay you by Letter of Credit direct to your bank. These LCs don't bounce—once wired to your bank, the money is yours.
- Overseas firms stay in business for years. If they like your service, they'll keep ordering, again and again. Each sale is easier for you!
- You have a bright future in exporting because the entire world is getting richer and better able to afford imported

items of various types. And you can get started for just pennies because postage is still cheap!

Expand to a Larger World

Some BWBs don't like to work with items to export. If you're one of these, I respect you. At least you know what you like and don't like.

Can you still get started on just pennies in an international mail-order business? Yes, you *can*. How? Go into the *licensing business.*

In the licensing business you act as a middle person to:

1. Find overseas firms seeking to use a patent, copyright, or tradename to make money from it.
2. Get a domestic firm to allow the overseas firm to use its patent, copyright, or tradename for a percentage of each sale made using one of these rights.
3. Collect a percentage of the percentage (usually 10% of 10%) for yourself as a fee for arranging the deal.

What kinds of products might you license overseas firms to use? There are thousands. Here are just a few examples:

• Electronics items of many different types (computers, integrated circuits, chips, etc.)
• Engines, boilers, pumps, and many other machines
• Books songs, plays, poetry, etc.

Again, as with exporting, you should pick the item you want to work with. Then you'll become an expert on it. People will refer others to you when they hear of someone seeking your type of licensed item. For a large view of licensing, see the book *How to Make a Fortune as a Licensing Agent,* listed at the back of this book.

Remember, though: You *can* get started for just pennies. And your mind can make you rich in this business as you develop new ideas and new ways to work out licensing deals that everyone benefits from—including you!

Widen Your Product Line

The other side of exporting is importing. Many people make fortunes in importing. How? Just think of the millions of:

- Autos, trucks, vans, and buses
- Cameras, VCRs, TVs, radios
- Boats, aircraft, trains, etc.

that are imported around the world. In importing, as in exporting, everyone benefits. Thus, money is made by the:

- Manufacturer of the item
- Importer of the item (you)
- Seller of the item (which could be you if you sell direct to customers, or a store or retail chain).

You must be careful when you go into importing to have a market for the item *before* you import. Why? For a number of good reasons. These are:

- If you don't check the market beforehand, you may find you have a garage full of digital watches (or whatever you imported) that no one wants.
- Prices charged by your competition may be much lower than you can charge. So you *must* check before you import. Again, you may find you have a sack full of dolls you imported that no one will pay the price you need for them. How many dolls can a child play with at once?

If you do decide to make importing your source of a million-dollar fortune, keep these facts in mind:

- It's safer to import industrial items needed by businesses than consumer items, where there may be intense competition.
- You can get an easy estimate of demand from companies needing industrial items. Consumer item estimates are more difficult to get because people often change their interests or needs. So you must be careful to get as wide a view of consumer demand as possible *before* you import any product. Otherwise, you may be the proud owner of that garage full of digital watches we mentioned earlier.

One popular consumer import item is covered by the general term *leather goods*. These goods include wallets, belts, handbags, shoulder bags, ski gloves, motorcycle gloves, travel bags, garment carriers, and briefcases. So you see, you have a wide range of items you might import under just one category—leather goods.

To be sure you have a ready market for such items *before* placing your order for imports:

1. Contact local stores by mail, telephone, or in person to get advance orders.
2. Sell to such outlets using catalogs or brochures supplied by the manufacturer free to you.
3. Get a deposit from the retailer so you're sure the order is a firm one.

Instead of taking on the responsibility of importing yourself, you can become a *distributor* for an overseas supplier. Thus, in the case of the leather goods above, you would be the local salesperson for one or more overseas manufacturers of leather goods.

You get the orders—again by mail, phone, or in person. But instead of paying for the imports yourself, the manufacturer pays for them. Your earnings will be lower since the manufacturer will pay only a commission on each sale to you. But your risk is much less!

Why? Because if you wind up with a garage full of items, they belong to the manufacturer. All you have to do is arrange for the items to be shipped back to the manufacturer—who pays all costs.

Again, you're working with people—the manufacturer and the buyer. They will help you build your riches because you serve them. Winning them to your cause is a big step toward your million-dollar fortune—starting right now.

Be Different—and Win Big

But suppose that import-export doesn't turn you on? What other ways might you use to build your million-dollar fortune? There are thousands of ways to make money today, working through other people. Here are a few ways you might want to consider. Or these ways may suggest others that appeal to you:

- Own your own travel agency. You can make big profits providing travel services to people and firms. You can either buy an existing travel agency or start your own. For a low-cost way to start making money from the travel business, see the book *Travel Free,* listed at the back of this book.
- Rent a used car dealership. You get the complete facility—office, lot, garage, etc. People will come to you to buy a used car because they know what the specialty of the dealership is — namely, used cars.
- Run bus tours to popular resorts. You don't even have to own the buses—you can lease them. You transport your customers from a local area to the resort early in the day and return them in the evening. Profits can be enormous.
- Get into vending machine millions! Today there are vending machines for almost every product needed by people. Get your machines in "action" areas and you'll clink your way to a million-dollar fortune! Have people place the machines, collect the coins or bills, and you'll make big money quickly and easily.
- Run a health club. In today's health and figure-conscious world, there are millions to be made from well-managed health clubs. Some clubs are even available with the financing in place. This means you won't need any funds of your own to get started.
- Own a 1-hour film developing center and branch out into several more centers in your area. You need only unskilled help since the machines do all the work. Locate near where people shop or get off public transportation lines and you'll reap big rewards every day!
- Help people get signature loans by mail. All you do is match borrower and lender—all by mail. Loans from $1,000 to $35,000 are available to those who qualify. Your fee (called a commission) may come from the borrower or lender, depending on how you set up the deal. See the *Mail Order Loan Success System,* listed at the back of this book for the exact steps to get started.
- Help people get first mortgage loans for homes, condos, and one- to four-family properties and earn up to 6.5 points. Thus, on a $500,000 mortgage with a commission of 6.5

points, your fee will be $32,500! That's a nice way to start your million-dollar fortune search. You need only 31 such mortgage fees to bank your million dollars. In an active area, 31 deals can be put together in less than one year! And you can work without a license of any kind—other than your driver's license.

- Get into computer and business equipment leasing as a lease broker. You earn quick commissions because many businesses prefer to lease equipment instead of buying it. All you need do is help the business fill out a few pieces of paper and you're in business. Your commission is typically 5%. Turnaround time is fast, and you can go from one deal to another quickly. Items often leased through you will include minicomputers, personal computers, autos, vans, electronic typewriters, copying machines, etc. See the *Mini-Lease Kit* at the back of this book for more info on this excellent business.

People Are Your Hidden Resource

Every business today depends on people. You may be the loner I mentioned earlier. But you need people to help you earn your million-dollar fortune. You really can't get away from this fact of business life!

So start today—right here and now—to learn how to appreciate people more. See and appreciate:

- The skills that people can bring to your business
- The machines that people can put to work for you to make the items you'll sell
- The reliability and honesty of almost every businessperson who serves your company
- The loyalty of employees who work for you for years and protect your interests when the going gets tough.

Unless you really like, and appreciate, people, you'll take longer to build your million-dollar fortune. If you'd prefer it that way, I say—good. I won't argue with you. But there *is* a shorter and easier way—through the help of the people you really need. Use their skills, their loyalty, their reliability, and you can have your million-dollar fortune much sooner than you think! How do I know? Because I've done it. And I'm ready to help you—day or night—as close to you as your telephone or mailbox!

DAY 7

You're almost certain to meet roadblocks on your way to your million-dollar fortune. But most of these roadblocks are predictable. And they can all be overcome. Your mind can find one or more ways to overcome any business problem. By using your mind and by taking needed action now, you can start building a hassle-free million-dollar fortune. On Day 7 you see how—and where—to begin knocking down any barriers in your way.

CHAPTER 7

OVERCOME ALL ROADBLOCKS TO YOUR FORTUNE MILLIONS

WHEN YOU BUILD WEALTH you run into roadblocks. That's a given, as successful wealth builders say. But these roadblocks can be overcome—if you know how.

Typical roadblocks BWBs meet include these:

- Lack of money to buy, or start, a successful business of one's own
- Lack of cosigners, guarantors, or others to make getting money easier
- Lack of help from experienced people in the business deals the BWB enters
- Lack of know-how about the business or real estate the BWB seeks to acquire
- Lack of legal guidance for BWBs
- Lack of accounting guidance for BWBs
- Lack of strategic direction for the firm
- Lack of advertising advice and skills.

Now you will never face all these roadblocks at once! But a few of them may crop up now and then. You *can* get around such roadblocks yourself—if you know how. Let's take a look at each and see how you can successfully overcome it when—and if—you face it.

Lack of Money Can Be Overcome

Most BWBs I meet have excellent business ideas. What they lack is the money to get the idea rolling and making big bucks for them. Here's how to overcome the lack of money.

1. *Look* at why you can't get money. There *must* be a reason. Once you know this reason, you're in a better position to cure your money lack.
2. *Take* steps to overcome the reason for your lack of money. See the details below for actions you can take.

BWBs try to raise money in three basic ways—(1) by borrowing it, (2) by seeking venture capital, and (3) by trying to sell stock to the public. A fourth way—by using grants— is less popular. So we will concentrate on the first three ways for now. We'll start with loans and cover the others later.

Borrowing money is the most popular way for BWBs to start or acquire a business. The roadblocks you may run into when you try to borrow money for a business include:

- Lack of sufficient collateral
- Poor credit rating
- History of bankruptcy
- Too many inquiries on your credit record
- Any other reason an unwilling lender can give.

But don't let these roadblocks get you down. I've seen BWBs overcome every one of these problems hundreds of times. Like this reader, who writes:

> I learned how to borrow $1 million from Ty. But I did not know what to do with it, totally, and how to keep the investments together. I presently own three houses which are income-producing, all in the $230,000 range, in Canada. And I have six rental houses in Florida; none are under $50,000 in value. Plus I have three extra pieces of land to build on. None of the experience, ambition, or entrepreneurship would have been possible without IWS and Ty Hicks.

Let's take a look at the common turn-down reasons above and see how you can overcome each one. While you may not use the method I give you, it might suggest ideas that work for you.

How to Overcome Loan Turn-Downs

You can't be afraid of trying to convince a lender to change a borrowing decision. Why? Because the lender will respect you if you can turn a *no* to a *yes*. So try to use any of the following ways to overcome loan turn-downs:

Reason Given

WAYS TO OVERCOME THE TURN-DOWN

Lack of enough collateral

1. Rent collateral from others; or borrow collateral from relatives or business associates.
2. Get one or more cosigners among friends, relatives, or business associates.
3. Use a "reverse-flip"—assign the business item you're buying with the loan as part, or full, collateral for the loan. Give full title to what you repay to your lender in the event you default.

Poor credit rating

1. Get a cosigner with a superb credit rating.
2. Give full details on why you're not the cause of the poor credit rating, if that is the case for you—which it often is. (For example, an angry spouse may have run up bills that were not repaid and were charged—wrongly—to you).
3. Start rebuilding your credit rating right now by charging what you can and then paying for it instantly.

History of bankruptcy

1. Explain to the lender what caused you to go bankrupt. Keep in mind that a medical bankruptcy (one caused by excessive medical bills in your family) is *never* thought to be as bad as other types of bankruptcies.
2. Use the "reverse-flip" listed above—it can really work for bankrupts.
3. Buy on the basis of "contact of sale"—that is, you don't own what you're buying until you reach a certain payment level for

the item. And if you fail to pay in full, the item bought goes back to the lender with all payments you made credited to the lender as though made by the lender.

Too many credit inquiries

1. Most credit reporting services "flush out" inquiries after a certain period of time. And there is a movement afoot to force an automatic removal after a certain specified time period. Find out from your lender which credit reporting agency was used; then ask how long inquiries are kept on file before being removed. Wait out the time until they're removed; then apply again.
2. If most of the inquiries on your record have not resulted in credit being granted, write the credit bureau, pointing out this fact. Ask that the inquiries be removed. Then apply again for the loan you need— after the inquiries are removed.

Other reasons

1. Get a written copy of the reason for the loan turn-down. Evaluate it and decide if you can get it reversed. For example, if the reason given is: "Employment history too short," go back to the lender and give info on your previous job history, if it's longer. Or if the reason is: "Residence rental too short," do the same for your earlier rentals.
2. Get legal help when the reason given is incorrect or inaccurate. Lenders are required to change wrong info in their files because the data can be harmful to you if not corrected.

The whole key to dealing with lenders who give you double-talk on loan rejection is:

- Correct any errors the lender makes.
- Be willing to write, call, or meet with lenders to state your position and get your loan.

• Be polite and businesslike at all times—but get your way!

Remember: Just because lenders have money doesn't mean they're perfect. Lenders can—and do—make mistakes. And most will gladly correct such errors when they're pointed out. But you must have the courage to do so. Then you'll overcome borrowing roadblocks faster than you might think. Just as this reader writes:

> The loan was accomplished here in Southern California very easily with the help of your newsletter. The names of people and companies requesting our package from our ad were terrific and an added plus benefit for future use.

As a last resort, you can try borrowing from IWS, using the loan program detailed in an earlier chapter. Our loans are geared to the BWB. So it's possible that you might get a loan from us after other lenders turn you down. We can't— of course—and don't say we'll make every loan sent to us. But we *do* promise to look it over carefully and give you a fast answer with *no* double-talk!

Where to Find Cosigners and Guarantors

A cosigner on a loan application can get you a loan you couldn't get on your own. So having a cosigner can be an important step toward your future wealth. To find a cosigner, look to:

• Relatives—parents, brothers, sisters
• Friends—good, and not-so-good
• Business associates in all fields
• Professional cosigner finding services.

Don't be bashful about going to friends, relatives, or business associates to find a cosigner. After all, what are these people for, if they can't help you? Surely, good friend, you'd be willing to help a friend or business associate—if you thought they had a good business idea.

Professional cosigner finding services look for a cosigner for you for a small fee. While such services cannot guarantee to find you the cosigner you seek, they do guarantee to publicize your need widely. Any deal you work out with the cosigner does not involve the finder. Typical fees you'll pay a cosigner *after* you obtain your loan are:

- Up to $1 million, 5% of the loan amount you obtain
- Up to $2 million, 4% of the loan amount you obtain
- Up to $3 million, 3% of the loan amount you obtain.

This is a one-time fee. It can be paid in full at the time you obtain your loan. Or it can be paid out over a period of time—usually the loan term. You'll pay one-third of the fee when you get your loan and the two-thirds balance over the life of the loan.

For one such professional finding service, see the *Global Cosigners and Money Finders Association,* listed at the back of this book.

There are a number of guarantor organizations that will get you a loan guarantee—for a fee. What's the difference between a cosigner and a loan guarantor? It's this:

- A cosigner has equal responsibility to repay the loan you get. A guarantor guarantees to repay just that portion of the loan you do not repay. So the guarantor has less exposure in the event of default—unless you go broke before the first payment is made. This rarely happens to BWBs who are careful in their deals.

The only complaint I have about commercial guarantors is that they charge a rather high fee—typically $5,000—before the loan is obtained. While such a fee may be justified, based on the work done, I strongly recommend to *all* my readers:

- Never pay a front fee before a loan is obtained. A reasonable fee is acceptable *after* the loan is obtained using the commercial guarantor. But a fee of the amount mentioned above paid prior to getting the loan is unacceptable, in my view.

Why are "front fees," "advance fees," and similar payments so undesirable? For a number of proven reasons, namely:

- Advance fees are often not earned—that is, the person

or organization receiving the fee does not perform the work for which the money is paid.

- It is often impossible for the BWB to recover the advance fee because the person or firm receiving the money has spent it and doesn't have any money to repay the person seeking the loan.
- Advance fees discourage hard work. Why? Once a person is paid, there's less incentive to work hard to achieve a goal—namely serving the customer.

Now when I talk about advance fees I'm thinking of amounts in the thousands of dollars. Smaller amounts—say up to $250—for services rendered are—in my opinion—acceptable. Why? Because if a person has to spend money for postage, phone calls, travel, and so on, some reimbursement is only fair.

To be completely safe, you should have a written agreement covering all fees over $100. Your agreement should detail what will be done for the payment, when reports will be made, and how much work you can expect from the person or firm receiving the fee.

Cosigners and guarantors *can* help you overcome the loan roadblock. Just be careful in your selection of cosigners and guarantors. Then you'll be happy with the results you get from such helpers.

Get Experienced People to Help You

When you're new to a certain business, you may be puzzled by certain questions that arise. Even the words used in the business may sound strange. When this happens, you may long for some help from people experienced in the business.

There's plenty of free help and advice available to small businesses. All it takes is a phone call and you can often get the answer you need. Free help you should look into includes:

- Small Business Administration (SBA) offers advice and guidance for small businesses in the form of both free and low-cost booklets. Contact your local SBA office after getting the phone number from your telephone book under the U.S. Government listing.

- Economic development offices of both cities and states offer much free assistance, including financing and venture capital, in some areas. You can find the address and telephone number of your economic development office in your local phone book in the state and city pages. You will often meet retired executives who are willing to help you, when you visit the economic development office in your state. These people may bring you the experienced advice that can help you achieve your goals.

- Your author—Ty Hicks—is ready to help with any business questions you may have. While I may not be able to answer every question you have, I usually can tell you where you can find the answer. That in itself may be worth the phone call!

When dealing with experienced people, be sure to listen carefully. You will probably learn much from such people. But keep these facts in mind:

- Some experienced people may be more cautious than need be for today's fast, turbulent, and competitive world. So listen, think, and then make your decision. For you know by now that *Your Mind Can Make You Rich!*

- Never be frightened by legal and license requirements of the business you want to enter. Why? Because if a license is required, you'll get it. And if you can't qualify for the license because of strict education and experience requirements, don't give up! You can almost always get around this requirement by hiring a properly licensed person to do the work for you. You'll earn a profit on their work while helping the person earn money in his or her chosen profession.

- Research can often reveal legitimate, legal loopholes in almost every license law. Find these loopholes and see if you can operate your business—legally—through one or more of the loopholes

A good example of the loophole that many BWBs use is in the law for real-estate brokers and mortgage brokers. All 50 states have such real-estate laws. These laws are similar from one state to another. Typically, an important loophole you might want to use is:

- Attorneys do *not* need a real-estate brokers license to participate in real-estate deals. So your attorney can often function for you, eliminating the need for you to have a broker's license.

Another important loophole that many BWBs overlook in the real-estate law is this one. Be sure to read it carefully:

- If you wish to operate as a Financial Broker or Financial Consultant and contact your local County Clerk, you'll probably be told you need a Real-Estate Broker's license. This is incorrect—if you can become the loan representative of a bank, credit union, savings and loan association, industrial lender, or other lender willing to lend money to people in the state. For such reps, *no* license is required! Why? Because every state wants to encourage lenders to do business in their borders—that is, lend money to residents and firms in the state. Requiring a license of loan reps would chase lenders out of the state! That's one result *no* state seeks. So they let people be Financial Brokers and Financial Consultants without any license (except a simple no-exam business registration for a few bucks).

Be sure to have an attorney check out your state's real-estate law for you. In almost every case you'll find that the above exemption from a license requirement *does* exist. It's just another example of getting experienced people to help you do better in your business by overcoming roadblocks.

Lack of Know-How Can Always Be Overcome

Knowledge is power. This is especially true today in this age of information. Just recognizing this can be a valuable bit of know-how for yourself.

Getting know-how about *your* business can often remove the need for help from experienced people. *You* become your own expert. While you must be very careful not to try to be your own doctor, lawyer, or accountant, you can:

- Often save money and time by getting important facts together to present to your professional advisor
- Understand better what your professional recommends that you do
- Be less fearful of the outcome of threats from outside groups or people because you know what limitations are placed on their actions.

You can get plenty of help from the books and kits listed at the back of this book. And, of course, there are other books and courses that can help you. The main points to keep in mind are:

- In business and real-estate moneymaking, your learning will be a lifelong process.
- Learning can be both fun and profitable. Forget dreary schools and schoolbooks—today's learning materials are easy to master and can put big bucks into your pockets! Remember—your mind can make you rich.

To show you what I mean, just look at this recent phone call from a reader in California who says (using the word *ideas* for *know-how*):

I bought a card and novelty store with no cash down, using your ideas. Since my credit is not large enough to handle the loan, the seller found a guarantor for me. The cost is 3.5% of the loan on the business but the promissory notes that I signed are not secured by the business. This means I can use the business as an asset for other loans I might need in the future.

The price of the business is $185,000, which is the amount the guarantor is covering. The sales of the business run $165,000 per year in just 600 sq ft of floor space. My net take-home will be $75,000 per year. Rent is only $1,200 per month. I plan on spending a few days a week in the store at the start; after that it will be just a few hours a week that I'll be there.

The most important thought for you to get from this section of the chapter is:

- Lack of know-how can always be overcome. Once you start getting the info you need, you'll start a lifelong search for money-making facts that will improve your income and your life.

Two readers who prove this write:

After reading a few of your books I applied at a bank for a business loan and got it. The loan was paid back early and I'm now finishing off a personal loan with them. I'm a BWB and I'm enjoying it.

And

Since I started with the *International Wealth Success* newsletter one year ago, I've taken over 31 income apartments.

Get Good Legal and Accounting Advice

In your own business you'll need legal advice in varying amounts, depending on the nature of your activities. But in every business you'll need regular accounting advice so you comply with the various tax laws—federal, state, and city.

Neither type of advice need be costly. You can get good advice at low cost if you learn as much as you can about the legal and tax aspects of your business. For example, each type of business has its own unique legal and tax aspects. Learning these on your own can help you assemble info and data for your attorney and accountant. This can save a lot of time for your professional. This means that your fees will be lower because these people bill on a time basis. Once the clock starts, your fees start to climb.

Suppose you're thinking of going into mail order/direct mail. The legal aspects you should face relate to the:

- U.S. Postal Service
- Federal Trade Commission (FTC)
- Better Business Bureau (BBB)
- Your state Attorney General (AG)
- Your state consumer protection group.

But if your business is in the field of real estate, the legal aspects you face relate to the:

- State Real-Estate Department

- Local tax assessor's office
- State tax assessor's office
- Insurance company policy department (for fire and liability coverage)
- Title search company (for a clear title guarantee)
- Mortgage lender's loan department.

Getting to know as much as you can about these, and other, regulatory and controlling groups can help you and your professionals. I'm not suggesting that you become a lawyer or accountant. Instead, you'll benefit by learning as much as you can about the laws and rules surrounding your business. Then you can *help* your professional, instead of being helplessly dependent on his or her opinions.

And every business, of course, must deal with the Internal Revenue Service. Your accountant will be the one who deals with and talks to the IRS for you. Again—though—you should know as much about the tax laws as possible! Why? Because:

- Accountants can—and do—make mistakes
- By knowing the tax laws you can check on your accountant's work and decisions
- You thereby might avert a costly penalty or interest charge.

In saying that professionals can make mistakes I'm *not* being critical. Instead, I fully respect lawyers and accountants. But I like to check their work because—after all—they're dealing with *my* money. I have a lot more affection for my money than they do. So I check their work. And in doing so I learn more. Why? They really know more than I do!

You can learn a lot about taxes and small business operation by contacting the IRS. They have a number of free booklets covering various aspects of business taxes. Get copies of these and read them carefully. You'll get an excellent education in both business and taxes.

One point that will come across to you is that taxes on a business are *not* a penalty. Instead, taxes are expenses a business pays to keep our government going. Every business benefits from various types of government help. So the business has to pay something for this help. That something is taxes.

Direct Your Firm to Success

You can steer your firm to success. How? By planning for the future right now! While most small businesses avoid planning, you really can't grow big without effective planning.

In the lingo of high-level business planners, you take strategic control of your firm when you plan its future. What most BWBs find hard is figuring out where they want to direct their business for its future success. Let's see if we can help you with this aspect of building your million-dollar fortune.

Your objective in being in business is to make money. But there's more to it than just money. Suppose you publish newsletters and kits, as I do. Here are my strategies for the business:

1. Develop needed newsletters and kits based on what we perceive and what people tell us is needed in the field of making money.
2. Prepare these newsletters and kits in such a way that they are:
   a. Easy to understand
   b. Simple to use
   c. Factually accurate
   d. Regularly updated
3. Rely on quality, early delivery, and personal help for all buyers to build loyalty to the company and to its officers and employees.
4. Expand the product line as new needs develop. Keep up with the needs of people seeking to make money in a business of their own.
5. Monthly, review the offerings of competitors to see if they have new products that better meet the needs of the market than ours do. If any competitors come up with a better product than ours, develop a new one that's better than theirs.
6. Offer the unique product—Direct Loans to Customers— to as wide a group as possible. Keep improving this unique product, which is not currently offered by any other similar firm, by:

   a. Reducing interest rates charged
   b. Extending the length of loans made
   c. Making qualifying easier
   d. Accepting simpler collateral.

There you have the strategic directions of one firm. You can base the growth strategies of *your* firm on similar goals, namely:

- Products or services meeting a definite need
- Emphasis on quality, delivery, personal service
- Attention to changing needs of the market
- Analysis of the competition on a regular basis and action to meet competitive thrusts
- Constant improvement of your unique product or service so it gives more to your customers.

So don't let the various strategy and planning terms throw you off! What you're aiming at is better service for your customers. This—in turn—delivers more profits to your bank account. And these profit dollars soon grow into your million-dollar fortune—the whole objective of your work!

Strong strategies and good business plans *do* work. How? The way they did for this reader, who writes:

> Thank you for your help in reviewing my business plans that I sent you on my company. I have now successfully acquired the $4-million loan I was seeking to start my new company. I really want to thank you for all your help. I am now on my road to success.

Good Advertising Brings Strong Results

There are few businesses that can get along without advertising. Your business will almost surely need good ads to bring in the big bucks. Knowing this, how can you get good ads? There are several ways:

1. Write the ads yourself. Plenty of small business people do write their own ads. But this takes time, skills, and creativity.
2. Hire an ad copywriter. Explain what you want, which

features of your product will sell most strongly, and what
you'll charge for the item or service.
3. Employ an ad agency to do all the work for you. After
a few meetings the agency will go away, work on your
ad, and then return with the finished copy. You get
professional results. But the cost will be higher than the
first two methods.

Which way is best for you? I really can't say until I know
your product, where you want to advertise it, what its price
is, etc. But my experience shows:

- It's fun, informative, and eye-opening to write your own
ads at the start. You get to know your product or service
better. And you see what features can be emphasized to
generate the largest sales.
- Once you've written the ad yourself, it's wise to have it
reviewed by a professional copywriter. This will usually
cost about $300, compared to $2,000 to write the ad from
scratch.
- Hiring an ad agency won't come until later in your business
life. Why? It's expensive—that's why!

Why is it important for you to write—or have written—
a good ad? For a number of million-dollar reasons, such as:

- You can run a good ad profitably for years. It will make
money every time you run it.
- A poor ad will "bomb out"—lose money—from the first
time you run it. Wouldn't you rather make money than
lose it?
- A good ad can bring in other business to you on what
mail-order/direct -mail people call the "bounceback."
That's where people order other items once they see the
first one you send them from the ad.

To prove that you can get rich from a good ad, I'm
reviewing the money status of a few wealth builders I know.
Here's a quick summary:

- One of these wealth builders flies his own twin-engine
plane, which he bought brand new. It has all the radio
and navigation gear that can be crammed into such a plane.
What paid for this plane? Just four great magazine ads

this wealth builder runs in magazines month after month. Cost of the plane? At least $500,000.

- Another wealth builder who runs great ads almost every month has a beautiful horse farm covering many hundreds of acres. He enjoys keeping his feet in the stirrups, instead of on the foot pedals of an airplane. Cost of this farm? At least $1.5 million.

I could go on. But I think you get the point. A good ad can bring in millions if you keep running it in the right publications. So start right now to get the right ad written for your product or service. The best ads—I find—are those that:

- Give specific facts to your reader
- Show the reader that you understand what problems the reader is trying to solve because you faced—and successfully solved—the same types of problems
- Offer a bonus item (I find two or three bonus items better than just one) for ordering now
- Allow the use of credit cards to order what you're offering
- Provide an 800 number for fast, easy ordering
- Give a quick response to every order.

In our loan programs that we offer readers (and nonreaders) of our newsletter, *International Wealth Success,* we promise a loan decision in one hour. Readers call and ask:

"... How long will it take to get a decision on my loan application?" My reply is "One hour." The usual next remark is: "How long did you say?" I reply—again—"One hour." And the next question is: "How long?" Yet all of this is given in our material. But—I guess—people skip over the one hour aspect of the material. So be sure to give your readers as much info in your ads as you can. Then they'll know in advance what they will get when they order your item or service.

Good ads need not be painful to write. Most good ads almost plead to be written. Why? Because people so often ask the same question that you say to yourself, "I'll write the ad so it answers the question I'm asked most often." Thus, the above loan ad might read:

One Hour Loan Decision! Is It Possible? Yes it *is*! If you apply for a loan as a subscriber (or nonsubscriber) of our newsletter. We promise to give you a *yes* or no answer to your loan application within one hour after we receive it! Your answer will either be called to you by telephone, if you wish. Or we'll send it to you by mail.

While we can't guarantee that you'll get a loan, we *DO* guarantee to give you your answer in one (1) hour—or less!

That's the headline and first few paragraphs of the ad. It goes on from there to other details, such as:

- Types of loans made (business and real estate)
- Loan period (1 day to 7 years)
- Interest rate (12% simple; 6% simple for emergency loans)
- Repayment (principal and interest monthly; or interest only monthly with principal at the end of the loan)
- Collateral required (all loans need some type of collateral).

You can see that an ad like this gives its readers the details they want. Then they can decide if they want to reply.

If you can afford a copywriter to write your ad, get that kind of help. It will make your ads much more profitable. And that—good friend—is the only reason for a BWB to advertise—to make money! It's a great way to build your million-dollar fortune without a lot of hassle.

Someday I'd like to have you help my staff open the mail we get from the many ads we run. I'll be glad to pay you for your time as you:

- Use a letter-opening machine to slice the tops off envelopes.
- Take checks and money orders from envelopes.
- Mark on the outside of the envelopes the item ordered and the amount enclosed.
- Note whether the check is a "regular" one—i.e., a personal or business check, or a money order.
- Mark on the envelope the date of the deposit of the regular check so we know how long to wait for the check to clear before we ship the item (*not* all checks clear—some bounce worse than a rubber ball).
- Assemble the envelopes for the typists so the labels for the packages can be typed.

You'd have great fun doing this work. Why? Because there's nothing more enjoyable than counting the money that comes in every day!

Also, we save every piece of business mail we get for five years. With the actual envelope on hand we can easily reconstruct every order. Why? Because we have:

- The mailing date from the postmark
- The place mailed from
- Name and address of the person placing the order
- Lack of a name and address—some folks forget to include these important details when ordering something! Crazy but true. With the envelope on hand for five years, we can easily prove to anyone anything!

So start now with good ads for your products or services. It's one of the best ways for you to make money today. And it can easily put you in the million-dollar fortune class. Could you ask for anything more?

Roadblocks Teach You How to Win

Don't let roadblocks get you down! Overcoming the roadblocks every business meets teaches you how to win. But in case I haven't convinced you, I'll let you in on the Ty Hicks Million-Dollar Fortune Building Secret for Overcoming Roadblocks. What's that secret? It's simple:

> *Sit down right now with pencil and paper and list all the roadblocks you can think of that might occur in your present or future business. Then list what action you will take to overcome each roadblock. This is called "Potential Problem Analysis" by a group of experts that teach people in large corporations how to win. You can use the same approach in the smallest business.*

Here are some typical roadblocks you might face in a new or going business. They may suggest to you the roadblocks you could face in your future business. But if they're not exactly what you have in mind, just change them to suit. Thus:

Potential Roadblock	**WAYS I WILL HANDLE IT**
Lack of enough cash flow to pay bills	Get loan that I set up in advance with a line of credit from _____ Bank.
Complaint from customer about service	Contact customer quickly; find out what is wrong; take steps to correct.
Loss of important workers	Line other possible workers; keep updated list of names and phone numbers for quick contact.
Sudden, fierce competition	List and study all competitors; see what they're doing that we can do better, cheaper, faster. Introduce new products or services to meet latest competition.
Large fall off in sales	Advertise and publicize products and services in short-deadline publications (newspapers, weekly magazines, etc.). Do quick mailings to hot prospects.
Environmental disaster beyond our control	Diversify into another business that is not affected by the disaster; get main business away from disaster area, if possible.

Once you list roadblocks and how you'll get around them, you'll sleep better. Why? Because you'll see that your mind can make you rich! It can help you overcome the typical roadblocks met in any business.

And if you can't figure out a way to get over a roadblock you face, just give me a ring. I'll be glad to help you, if you subscribe to my newsletter or use one of my kits. This service is free and I'll spend as many hours with you as you need to conquer the roadblocks.

Just *remember this:* You can overcome all roadblocks on the way to your fortune millions. All you need do is use your mind and start taking needed actions—for your own success! *Your mind can make you rich!*

DAY 8

Results—every working day—are what build your million-dollar fortune. Today you see how to get the results you seek—using your mind to build your riches. Since wealth building is a mind-based activity, the more you believe that your mind can make you rich, the greater the chances of you becoming wealthy—sooner! So let's start getting the important results you seek—and need—on the way to your million-dollar fortune!

CHAPTER 8

BE A RESULTS PERSON EVERY DAY—AND MOVE AHEAD

YOUR MILLION-DOLLAR FORTUNE can be built only one way. That way? By getting *results* every day of the week for your efforts. Without results you have nothing. So you must aim for your desired results every day of the week!

Results Are the Key to Your Success

The result of all your efforts to build wealth will be your million-dollar fortune. Aiming at this result gives your life direction and purpose. It will also put big chunks of money into your bank. And that—good friend—is the result you seek!

How do you see a result before you produce it? You use your mind. Why? Because your mind can make you rich! Seeing a result in your mind gives you the direction in which to go to obtain the result you seek. So building wealth is really a mind-based activity.

What results might you seek in building your million-dollar fortune? Here are typical results BWBs often seek:

- Getting information on lenders who may help you
- Finding an accountant to do your business books
- Registering your company name with the county clerk
- Obtaining a loan for a needed amount of money
- Finding a stockbroker to take your company public

- Getting a specific amount of venture capital for your business
- Obtaining a grant for your business.

Note that each of these results is specific. It isn't vague or foggy. For example:

> *There's nothing vague about "Obtaining a loan of a needed amount of money." Why? Because when you obtain the loan, you* have *the money (or a check) in your hand. So the result you sought has been reached and you are one step closer to your million-dollar fortune. So be sure to seek* specific *results!*

Some BWBs fool themselves by making an intermediate result their final result. So what's the outcome? They never reach their final goal—a million-dollar fortune. As one reader told me:

> I'm forever hearing from people about their "near misses." I'm really not interested in these. What I want to hear are actual success stories where people achieved a specific result they aimed for. I see people getting excited when they get a loan approval from a lender. While it's nice to get an approval from a lender, that's *not* the final result the BWB seeks. What *is* sought is a check from the lender in the amount of the loan that the BWB needs. Then the result the BWB seeks is obtained!

Set Up Daily Goals for Yourself

Building a million-dollar fortune using your mind is a series of small steps. Each step leads to a needed result. To achieve the results you seek:

1. Set up daily goals for yourself.
2. Make each goal a specific result you need to build your million-dollar fortune.
3. Direct your efforts each day toward reaching the result you seek for that day.
4. If you don't reach the day's goals, slide the unmet ones to the next day. Analyze why you didn't reach certain goals each day. If the reason is within yourself (such as

not making a needed phone call, failing to write a letter,
etc.) take steps to prevent this from happening again.
Drive yourself to meet your daily goals!

Use your daily business calendar to list that day's goals.
Then keep your calendar in front of you each day. Check
off in red each goal you reach. Aim at having *all* goals checked
every day.

At my firm, IWS, we have a 128-page calendar that we
give free to our subscribers when they renew their newsletter
subscription. Called a "Pocket Pal," this calendar has space
for each day's goals. It slips into your pocket or purse easily
and goes where you go. Get yourself this calendar or a similar
one. It can work miracles in helping you get results.

To show you how some BWB readers use a results-driven
aproach to build their million-dollar fortune, I'll give you
three recent examples. These BWBs got results in the areas
of (1) public money for their company needs, (2) venture
capital to finance a startup, and (3) a business grant to fund
a needed public service. Let's take a look at each.

Control Results to Generate Millions

You can raise millions for your company from the public—
if you control the results of your efforts. And you can get
this money even if:

- Your firm has not made one sale
- Your firm is just starting
- Your firm has only one employee—yourself
- Your firm is only a gleam in your eye
- Your firm has little experience in its field.

"How can this be?" you ask. It can be because the investing
public is willing to risk money on new firms that may turn
out to be the next Apple Computer, Xerox, Hewlett-Packard,
etc. Who knows—your firm may become the largest one of
its type in the world—making millionaires out of its early
investors, and yourself! So the willingness to take a chance
is always there.

What do you need to go public? You need results! These results are in several simple forms and steps, namely:

1. A business plan (called a *prospectus*) detailing your firm, its market, its management, its competition, and the amount of money needed.
2. An application to the Securities and Exchange Commission (SEC) for approval of your prospectus.
3. An acceptance by a stockbroker to sell the securities in your firm to either the general public or to a private group.
4. A successful sale of your securities to raise the money you seek for your firm.

Each of these four steps has a result as its goal. And I can guarantee you this: If you achieve each of these results your firm *will* have money to get started, expand, or otherwise grow. Could you ask for anything more?

So let's put you into the business of getting money from the public—right now. It's really much easier than you think.

Get Your Business Plan Result

Your business plan/prospectus will follow a standard outline. Why? Because people are used to seeing the standard outline. Any variation from it makes them wonder. Further, the SEC has a suggested outline that's excellent. So you should not deviate from it, unless you have good reasons to do so.

The standard SEC outline for a prospectus is shown in Fig. 8-1. Use it when you write your business plan because you'll get two results for one effort, namely, (1) your needed prospectus, and (2) a business plan that anyone will feel comfortable reading.

Should you write your business plan yourself? My answer—which you may not like—is yes, you should! Why? For a number of good and proven reasons, namely:

• Writing your own business plan is eye-opening
• Because you learn more about your business
• And its market and competitors
• Than you ever thought possible

(Continued on page 176)

Fig. 8-1 *Prospectus Outline*

Regulation A

**GENERAL RULES AND REGULATIONS
UNDER THE SECURITIES ACT OF 1933.**

SCHEDULE I—INFORMATION TO BE INCLUDED
IN THE OFFERING
CIRCULAR REQUIRED BY RULE 256

The offering circular required by Rule 256, or statement required by Rule 257, shall be dated and shall contain the following information:

1. The following statement shall be set forth on the outside front cover page of the offering circular in capital letters in type as large as that used generally in the body of the circular:

   THESE SECURITIES ARE OFFERED PURSUANT TO AN EXEMPTION FROM REGISTRATION WITH THE UNITED STATES SECURITIES AND EXCHANGE COMMISSION. THE COMMISSION DOES NOT PASS UPON THE MERITS OF ANY SECURITIES NOR DOES IT PASS UPON THE ACCURACY OR COMPLETENESS OF ANY OFFERING CIRCULAR OR OTHER SELLING LITERATURE.

2. State the exact name and address of the issuer, the name of the State or other jurisdiction under the laws of which it was incorporated or organized and the date of its incorporation or organization.

3. a. Give the following information, in the tabular form indicated, on the outside front cover page of the offering circular on a per-share or other unit basis.

Offering price to public	Under-writing discounts or commissions	Proceeds to issuer or other persons

   b. If any of the securities are to be offered for the account of any person other than the issuer, give the name and address of each such security holder, the total amount he owns and the amount to be offered hereunder for his account.

   (Continued)

4. a. State the amount of securities to be offered pursuant to this regulation, the aggregate offering price to the public, the aggregate underwriting discounts or commissions, the amount of expenses of the issuer and the amount of expenses of the underwriters to be borne by the issuer, and the aggregate proceeds to the issuer or security holders for whose account the securities are to be offered.

   b. If the securities are not to be offered for cash, state the basis upon which the offering is to be made.

5. Describe briefly the method by which the securities are to be offered and if the offering is to be made by or through underwriters, the name and address of each underwriter and the amount of the participation of each such underwriter, indicating the nature of any material relationship between the issuer and such underwriter.

6. a. Furnish a reasonably itemized statement of the purposes for which the net cash proceeds to the issuer from the sale of the securities are to be used and the amount to be used for each such purpose, indicating in what order of priority the proceeds will be used for the respective purposes.

   b. Describe any arrangements for the return of funds to subscribers if all of the securities to be offered are not sold; if there are no such arrangements, so state.

7. Give a brief description of the securities to be offered pursuant to this regulation. Include the following information:

   a. In the case of shares, the par or stated value, if any; the rate of dividends, if fixed, and whether cumulative or noncumulative; a brief indication of the preference, if any; and if convertible, the conversion rate.

   b. In the case of debt securities, the rate of interest; the date of maturity, or if the issue matures serially, a brief indication of the serial maturities, such as "maturing serially from 1985 to 1995"; if the payment of principal or interest is contingent, an appropriate indication of such contingency; a brief indication of the priority of the issue; and if convertible, the conversion rate.

   c. In the case of any other kind of securities, appropriate information of a comparable character.

8A. Mining business. If the issuer is engaged or proposes to engage in mining or exploratory mining operations, briefly describe the business or proposed business of the issuer in accordance with the following instructions:

    a. Give the location and means of access to the mining properties now held or intended to be acquired and the nature of the title under which such properties are held or intended to be held. Indicate any known risks to which such title may be subject.

    b. Identify the principal metallic or other constituents of the deposits to be explored or developed and describe the characteristics of such deposits. No claim shall be made as to the existence of a body or ore unless it has been sufficiently tested to be properly classified as "proven" or "probable" ore, as defined below. If the work done has not established the existence of proven or probable ore, a statement shall be made that no body of commercial ore is known to exist on the property.

    c. The term "proven ore" means a body of ore so extensively sampled that the risk of failure in continuity of the ore in such body is reduced to a minimum. The term "probable ore" means ore as to which the risk of failure in continuity is greater than for proven ore, but as to which there is sufficient warrant for assuming continuity of the ore.

    d. If statements are made as to the existence of proven or probable ore, furnish separately for the information of the Commission copies of the pertinent maps and other supporting data, including calculations, with respect to such ore. Geologists' and engineers' reports, if used in an offering circular, shall be written in a clear and concise form.

    e. If the properties are known to have been previously explored, developed or mined by anyone and that fact or the results of such previous work is material, furnish information as to such work insofar as it is known and material.

8B. Oil or gas business. If the issuer is engaged or proposes to engage in the oil or gas business, briefly describe the business or proposed business of the issuer in accordance with the following instructions:

(Continued)

a. State the area and location of the various properties proposed to be developed or exploited by the issuer and the nature of the issuer's interest therein.

b. State the development which has occurred to date on or near the properties held. If no such development has occurred, a statement to that effect shall be made.

c. State (in tabular form), for all productive properties, net production of oil and gas to issuer's interest from each of the properties by years for the past 4 years prior to the latest year, and by months for the latest year, as well as the number of net producing wells owned by the issuer which contributed to the production during each of the time periods involved.

d. State the estimated future reserves net to issuer's interest in such properties which are proved.

e. If statements concerning geology or engineering are made, furnish separately for the information of the Commission copies of the pertinent reports and other supporting data. Geologists' and engineers' reports, if used in an offering circular, shall be written in a clear and concise form.

8C. Other business. If the issuer is engaged or proposes to engage in any business other than those specified in Items 8A and 8B, briefly describe the business or proposed business of the issuer in accordance with the following instructions:

a. State the nature of the issuer's present or proposed products of services, the principal market therefor and the length of time issuer has been in commercial production.

b. State the location and general character of the plants or other physical properties now held or presently intended to be acquired and the nature of the title under which such properties are held or proposed to be held.

c. If the issuer intends to exploit or develop any new invention or process, state how such invention or process is to be applied commercially and whether or not it is covered by any patent, issued or pending. Identify by serial number and date any applicable patents or patent applications.

d. Engineers' and other technical reports, if used in the

offering circular, shall be written in a clear and concise form.

9. a. Give the full names and complete residence addresses of all directors and officers of the issuer and of any person or persons controlling the issuer. If the issuer was incorporated or organized within the last 3 years, furnish similar information as to all promoters of the issuer.

b. State the aggregate annual remuneration of all directors and officers of the issuer as a group and the annual remuneration of each of the three highest-paid officers of the issuer.

c. Describe all direct and indirect interests (by security holdings or otherwise) of each person named in answer to (a) above (i) in the issuer or its affiliates and (ii) in any material transactions within the past 2 years or in any material proposed transactions to which the issuer or any of its predecessors or affiliates was or is to be a party. Include the cost to such persons of any property or services for which any payment by or for the account of the issuer has been or is to be made.

d. If the issuer was incorporated or organized within the last 3 years, state the percentage of outstanding securities of the issuer which will be held by directors, officers and promoters, as a group, and the percentage of such securities which will be held by the public, if all of the securities to be offered under this regulation are sold, and the respective amounts of cash (including cash expended for property transferred to the issuer) paid therefor by such group and by the public.

10. A brief description of all options or warrants presently outstanding or proposed to be granted to purchase securities of the issuer, including the names of the principal holders of such options or warrants, the cost of the options or warrants to them, the terms and conditions upon which they may be exercised and the price at which the securities may be acquired pursuant to such options or warrants.

11. Furnish the following financial statements of the issuer, or of the issuer and its predecessors, prepared in accordance with generally accepted accounting principles and practices. The statements required for the issuer's

(Continued)

latest fiscal year shall be certified by an independent public accountant or certified public accountant if the issuer has filed or is required to file with the Commission certified financial statements for such fiscal year; the statements filed for the period or periods preceding such latest year need not be certified.

a. A balance sheet shall be furnished as of a date within 90 days prior to the filing of a notification, or such longer period of time, not exceeding six months, as the Commission may permit at the written request of the issuer upon a showing of good cause therefor.

b. Statements of income, statements of source and application of funds, and statements of other stockholders' equity shall be furnished for each of at least two full fiscal years prior to the date of the statement furnished pursuant to paragraph (a) above, and for the period, if any, between the close of the last full fiscal year and the date of such statements, or for the period of the issuer's existence if less than the period specified above.

c. If the issuer meets the criteria for a development stage company specified in Rule 1-02 of Regulation S-X, additional information shall be included, as prescribed in Rule 5A-02 of Regulation S-X, in the financial statements required to be furnished under paragraphs (a) and (b)

(Amended, eff. April 15, 1972, Release 33-5225).
(Amended, eff. December 26, 1975, Release 33-5642.)
Excerpted from SEC "Regulation A."
For complete wording, see latest edition of the Regulation. This excerpt is provided here only as an example and should *not* be used in preparation of an actual prospectus.

- Making you a better-informed wealth builder
- Able to take a firm from small beginnings
- To a million-dollar fortune for yourself
- In a relatively short time.

Now you may not like to write. I understand this. So I'll make you an offer you can't refuse. What is my offer? It's this:

Subscribe to my newsletter, *International Wealth Success,* for two years ($48) and I'll write your business plan for you—

free of any charge! You will—of course—have to supply me
with info on your proposed business. But with that in hand
you need do no more than send it to me with a request that
I do your business plan. I promise to deliver it to you within
a week after I get your info. And if the business plan I write
for you isn't acceptable, you can easily mark it up and return
it to me for revision. Or you can do the revision yourself.
Then you'll have the result you seek—an accurate and well-
written business plan that can help you raise millions from
the public.

To show you that new, untried firms *can* raise money from
the public via a stock offering, I've included Fig. 8-2. In it
you'll see summaries of recent public offerings by a number
of new firms. As you'll see when you read these, money *can*
be raised for the new company from the public.

Current rules allow you to raise $5 million in your first
public offering during the first year. This amount may be
more than you need. If so, just reduce the amount you seek
to the level you need. You'll see that some of the firms in
Fig. 8-2 did just that. There's *no* rule against lowering your
money needs! Your company *must* be organized as a
corporation.

Fig. 8-2.   *Examples of Typical Summaries of Public Offerings.
(Courtesy Wall Street Syndicators)*

80,000 Units @ $6.00
_____, INC., was organized under the laws
of the State of Florida on August 11, 1986 for the purpose
of creating a vehicle to obtain capital to take advantage of
business opportunities. The company intends upon completion of this offering to seek potential business ventures which
in the opinion of management will provide a profit to the
company. (The principal use of the proceeds of this Offering
and the company's principal place of business will be within
the United States). Such involvement can be in the form of
the acquisition of existing businesses or the acquisition of
assets to establish businesses for the company. The company
has no understanding or arrangement to acquire any business
and has designated no specific geographic area, industry or
type of operation in which it will seek to operate. There
is and can be no assurance that the company will be able

to acquire an interest in any business, or that any activity of the company, even after such acquisition, will be profitable. Management of the company will have unlimited discretion in determining the business activities in which the company will become engaged. Present management of the company may or may not become involved as management in the aforementioned businesses and in the event that they do not, they will hire presently unknown and unidentified individuals as management for the aforementioned ventures.

The company is in the development stage and has not transacted any business other than organizational matters. The company at this time has no full time employees and no material assets.

Company Contact:
Address:
Underwriter: Company

7,500,000 Shares @ $1.00

_____, FUND, will engage in speculative transactions involving commodity interests including commodity futures contracts and forward contracts and other interests in commodities (including without limitation, options contracts on futures and cash commodities and foreign currencies) according to the trading strategies and the trading policies. The partnership will maintain a portion of its assets (initially approximately 50%) in Zero Coupons, which may be subject to margin calls. The partnership intends to purchase the Zero Coupons at a substantial discount from their face amount. The portion of the partnership's assets used to purchase Zero Coupons, and the maturity of the Zero Coupons purchased, will depend upon prevailing interest rates.

Company Contact:
Address:

Underwriter: _____ and Associates

150,000 Units @ $.75

_____, VENTURES, INC., was organized under the laws of the State of Delaware on March 3, 1986.

The company intends upon completion of this offering to seek potential business ventures which in the opinion of management will provide a profit to the company. Such involvement can be in the form of the acquisition of existing businesses and/or the acquisition of assets to establish businesses for the company. Present management of the company does not expect to become involved as management in the aforementioned businesses and will hire presently unknown and unidentified individuals as management for the aforementioned ventures.

Company Contact:
Address:

Underwriter: Company

Find a Suitable Brokerage House

The next result you seek is a brokerage house that agrees to sell stock in your firm without any advance payments. This means that the fees for the brokerage house will come out of the proceeds of the stock sale.

How do you find such a brokerage house? That's easy. You take these quick, simple steps:

1. Write—or have written—an Executive Summary describing your company. If you can't, or don't want to write this Summary, I'll be glad to do it for you under the same terms as those listed above for your business plan.
2. Write a letter to selected brokerage houses offering each the right to sell your stock. An example of such a letter is given in Fig. 8-3. Use this letter as given here. Or change it to suit your needs.
3. Send your letter to the brokerage houses you've picked. The best ones to pick are those that specialize in the offerings of new, untried firms. You'll find such firms listed in the book *Wall Street Syndicators*, listed in the back of this book.
4. Wait for the response. Most brokerage houses will give you a quick yes or no answer. If you get more than one yes answer, hold off agreeing to allow one firm to make

Fig 8-3.   *Typical Letter to Brokerage House Asking Them to Sell Your Shares.*

Your Company Name, Inc.
Your Address
Telephone No.

_____ , President
_____ Stockbrokers
_____
_____

Dear _____ :

Enclosed is an Executive Summary for _____ Corporation, which we would like to take public at an early date.

When you read the Executive Summary you will see that _____ Corporation has much promise. Its products are needed by millions of people throughout the world.

Further, the management team _____ Corporation has assembled is widely experienced in its field of business. And this team has strong plans for making the company grow into one of the most profitable in its field.

A complete Prospectus is available for your review. We will be happy to send it to you. Just call me at the above number, or write to me at the above address.

And if you have any questions before, or after, you see the Prospectus, I will be happy to answer them. We believe this is a great opportunity for your firm and ours. So we look forward to hearing from you soon.

Very truly yours,

Your Name, President

SS:stl

the sale until you've evaluated all offers. This way you can pick the best offer. With a promising company, you may get as many as six offers to take your firm public. So be ready to judge one offer against another.

Where you get multiple offers, the differences will usually be in the fees the brokerage house wants to charge. Your usual cost to go public will be about 12% of the amount raised. So if you raise $1 million, the cost will be $120,000. This means your firm would get $880,000 of money that never need be repaid. Further:

* There would be *no* monthly loan payments.
* *No* interest would be charged on the money you get.
* Your personal credit rating would not be marred if you failed to make money from the money.

So having the right brokerage house is important. Once you've picked the brokerage house to handle your deal, you'll be asked to sign an agreement. Do *not* sign anything until your attorney and accountant study the agreement. Then follow their advice as to any changes they suggest.

Sell Shares Yourself

If you want to save the 12% charge made by brokerage houses, you can sell shares in your own firm yourself. And any other officers in your firm can also sell shares in it. Selling shares yourself:

* Saves a big brokerage fee that can reduce the net proceeds to your company
* Allows you to get started sooner; you can use a typed prospectus instead of a printed one and save 30 to 40 days of time needed to raise money
* Puts you in closer touch with the people who will own shares in your corporation
* Allows you to sell large blocks of stock at one time to one investor to raise money in big chunks, instead of having it dribble in a few dollars at a time.

A number of our readers have gone public by writing their own prospectus, having it typed, and then selling the stock themselves. Most of these readers got the amount of money they sought. As one reader told me:

> I didn't think I could raise money for my Financial Brokerage Company by selling stock to others. But it was much easier than I thought it would be, once I wrote the Prospectus and typed it up. I used a number of diagrams in the Prospectus to show what my corporation was trying to do. Many buyers of my stock told me that the diagrams convinced them that the stock was a good buy.
>
> From the Financial Brokerage Company I moved on to a film production company. This firm has been highly successful in both fields and I'm truly glad I decided to sell stock on my own. You must, of course, enjoy selling. If you don't, then the best way to raise the money you need is to have a brokerage house sell the stock for you!

You can get a copy of the above Prospectus when you use our *Business Plan Kit,* described at the back of this book. You'll see the diagrams the reader mentions when you read the Prospectus. And the *Financial Broker Kit,* again listed at the back of this book, gives you many ideas on how to take any company public. *Remember:* The result of all your effort is the money your company gets. Raise the money and your results for the day will be great!

Get Venture-Capital Results Quickly

Venture capital also is money that never need be repaid. But you must have a business that promises strong future growth if you want to raise venture capital today. Typical businesses promising strong growth include:

- Electronics firms making semiconductors
- Computer hardware and software firms
- Aerospace and satellite manufacturers
- Advanced telephone and networking builders
- Medical and industrial laser firms
- Personal computer manufacturers, including clones

- Alarm system builders
- Certain low-tech firms serving growing markets—typical are supermarket, auto repair, fast-food, and entertainment companies.

Most BWBs start with low-tech companies, such as those mentioned above. A few I meet are in the hi-tech areas. If you're one of these, you can raise millions just with a short business plan. With low-tech products, you'll need a longer business plan that includes market projections.

The fastest way to get venture-capital results quickly takes just a few steps. These steps are:

1. *Define your business.* Is it low-tech or hi-tech? Once you know this, it's easier to pick a venture capital firm that might finance your business.
2. *Decide how much money you need.* This isn't as easy as it sounds! You *must* figure how much money you'll need for each step in the development of your business. To do this, sit down with pencil and paper and make some estimates of the amount you'll need for startup, salaries, equipment, rented offices and production facilities, etc. If your estimate doesn't add up to at least $500,000, consider getting a loan instead of venture capital. Why? Because at amounts under $500,000, the growth potential really isn't there for the ven cap firm. And growth is the name of their game—day and night!
3. *Contact by phone* selected venture capitalists. Ask if they'd be interested in hearing more about your _____ (*business type*) firm that needs (*money amount*) to get started, or to expand its current business. Then say, "We expect to grow (*no. of times*) in the next 5 years. Would you like to see an Executive Summary?" Keep trying until you find at least one, and preferably three, ven cap firms interested in your project.
4. *Write the same firms, if you prefer not to call.* Writing takes much longer, but some people prefer to write instead of calling. If you write, include the same info as in step 3 in your letter. Include a stamped, self-addressed envelope (SASE) to speed your answer.
5. *Send a copy of your Executive Summary* describing your business and its potential. Wait for a positive answer from the ven cap firm. If you have a business with strong growth

potentials, you're almost certain to get the venture capital you seek. Just use the quick-results steps—starting right now! *Remember:* The results you seek are venture capital in your firm's bank. So concentrate on that goal as you take these steps.

Reach Free-Money Results Quickly

There's really nothing like what people call "free money" to get you started earning money in your own business. Free money really isn't free. You *must* work to keep the money you get for a few pieces of paper.

But free money—usually called *grants*—has many interesting and attractive features. Thus, grants:

- Never need be repaid, if you do the work for which the grant was made
- Can be renewed with an injection of new money to you from the grantor
- May go on for years and years if the project needs more work on your part
- Will attract other grants if you do a good job and maintain cordial dealings with the grantor.

I've worked with many grantors. And my firm, IWS, Inc., makes grants to BWBs for worthy causes. Yet both large and small grantors have real problems finding suitable projects and people to whom they can make grants! Why is this? There are a number of reasons, such as:

- Many people don't even know that grants exist. You now know, if you didn't know before. Getting people to know, and understand, grants is a big job faced by every grantor.
- Some people don't want to go to the trouble to prepare a short letter telling what they want to do, who will benefit, and how much money is needed for how long. Million-dollar grants are made on the basis of a one- or two-page single-spaced typed letter. If this is too much work for someone, then they deserve not to get a grant of free money!
- Other people don't take time to find out what kinds of projects a grantor likes. For instance, at IWS we like small business projects that teach people about the great benefits

to everyone of our capitalistic system. So if a BWB comes to us with a well-prepared proposal for a grant to extol the benefits of capitalism, it's likely that the grant will be made—quickly and easily. We're looking for deals—not ordeals! So your short proposal should feature the benefits the grantor believes in promoting. Result for you? You *get* the free-money grant you seek.

I wish you could be at meetings with me when we "cry" over not being able to put our grant money to work. Since the purpose of every grant-making group is to get money out doing good, its directors worry when they can't put their money to work.

So help some "poor" grantor get some more sleep at night. Use the grantor's money for a worthwhile purpose. You'll be a hero to the grantor and your business associates. Just get that short one- or two-page proposal written—right now! Then get it off to a suitable grantor. See the grants kits at the back of this book for more info on free money. You'll get the results you seek when you have the right info on what to do. A grant can be your key to the million-dollar fortune you seek.

A number of my readers regularly obtain grants for their work. How can they be so successful? They:

- Tailor every grant request (proposal) to the grantor they've targeted
- Include every detail the grantor might seek in making a decision on the grant
- Call the grantor before they send the grant request to be sure the grantor is interested in what the person is doing for the grant.

Get Breakout Financing Results

Your mind can make you rich. Your mind can give you your million-dollar fortune. All you need to know is what to do. One approach is what I call *Breakout Financing*. It:

- Forces you into unusual ways to finance your wealth-building tasks
- Supplying you with different ways to get the money you need for your million-dollar fortune

- While getting you out of the run-around that some ill-informed bank clerks might give you if you tried to get Breakout Financing from a bank.

What do I mean by Breakout Financing to get the wealth results (a million-dollar fortune) that you seek? I mean financing obtained in any one or more of these six ways:

1. No-credit-check lenders
2. Private lenders seeking a good return on their money
3. Overseas lenders wanting to put excess funds to work
4. Credit unions—new to business lending—but aggressive
5. Asset-based lenders with millions to loan firms
6. Forming an offshore bank to attract capital

Each of these ways is a Breakout Method because it's not wrapped up in conventional lending rules. Such rules can shoot you down before you even show up for a loan interview or send an application to your lender. And each of these methods *can* get you the money results you seek. Let's see how—now!

No-Credit-Check Lenders

There *are* risk-taking lenders around. And you can work with them to build your million-dollar fortune. What does the lender mean when it advertises:

- No-credit-check loans
- Bankruptcy no problem
- Job history unimportant
- Poor credit/slow pay acceptable.

When you see such statements from a lender it means that this is a source of money that:

- Will—and can—take risks
- Has figured out how to cover possible losses
- Will probably charge higher interest rates on loans
- Can make loans to you quickly.

What does such a lender demand from you to make a loan? This type of lender will usually ask:

- That you put 20% to 25% down on any real estate you're buying with the borrowed money
- That you pay (at this writing when the prime rate is 10%) 16% interest on the loan you get
- That you pay as high as 6 points (6% of the loan) as fees for the loan.

Wow! you say. And I reply with the same—Wow! But the point is you *can* get a loan. And if you wheel and deal with the lender you may be able to get a big reduction in both the interest rate and the points. I know some "hard money" lenders (which is what such lenders are called) who charge only 2% over prime for interest and just two points for fees. How do you find such lenders? By looking! And IWS can help—if you subscribe to our newsletter.

Hard money like this *can* get you started making your million-dollar fortune. Why? Because you *do* get the results you seek—namely, the cash to start or buy the business you want. Thus, readers report:

- Buying a going business in the auto supplies field using hard money obtained through a home equity loan at 16% interest. Why the high rate? Because the borrower had poor credit, no job, and a record of slow pay on earlier bills. Yet his auto supplies business boomed and he was able to repay the loan in less than a year and get out from under the 16% interest charge! He got the *results* he sought—he was able to buy the business he wanted and he had the business repay the loan he used to buy it!
- Another reader used borrowed money to pay for an unusual mailing to sell a financial product. The usual return on such a mailing is 2%—that is, 2 sales for each 100 letters mailed. Using an unusual written aproach, this reader was able to get a 12% return (12 orders for each 100 letters mailed). That's six times the usual return. So even though hard money had to be used to finance the mailing, the results quickly repaid the loan. Again, the desired *results* are making this reader rich!

Get Results with Private Lenders

In borrowing money you have two basic types of lenders—*public* and *private*. The *public* lender is a bank, a mortgage company, a commercial finance company, etc. A *private* lender is a person, a company, or a group of people or companies that lend money for any business purpose. (*Remember:* Real estate *is* a business).

Why deal with private lenders instead of (or in addition to) public lenders? There are a number of good reasons for dealing with private lenders, such as:

- Greater speed in getting a loan decision
- Less paperwork to fill out for a loan
- More willingness to take a risk on a borrower
- Friendlier treatment by the lender.

Any private lender must abide by the state laws on interest. This means that you won't be charged a rate higher than that legally allowed. And most private lenders charge less than the state maximum rate of interest. Why? Then there's *no* chance that they'll be accused of usury—excessive interest.

I'm constantly in touch with dozens of private lenders. They're always looking for new deals. So they come to me to recommend new clients. And I'm glad to do so (for *no* points, fees, retainers, or any other charges) because it makes me feel good to help any BWB who subscribes to my monthly newsletter, *International Wealth Success*.

Here's a recent ad from one of the private lenders I follow. The actual phone number is not given since it may change before this book is printed. The ad reads:

> Private Mortgage $ Available. Short term only. Commercial & Residential. Any worthwhile purpose. Closing normally within 5 days. Brokers protected. Call 123-4567; ask for Ed.

Now there are private lenders who give long-term loans—typically up to 30 years. And these private lenders make loans for business deals of all kinds. Others do real-estate deals, as the above ad shows.

How can you contact private lenders? You can do so by reading the pages of the *IWS* newsletter mentioned above every month. And my *Money Watch Bulletin* (see the back of this book) also gives monthly names, addresses, and telephone numbers of private lenders.

Using a private lender can get you the results (money) you seek. And this private money can put you on the first step toward your million-dollar fortune.

Overseas Lenders Can Give You Money Results

Overseas lenders often want to break into new markets. So you can use such lenders for your Breakout Financing. Why might overseas lenders do the job you require and give you the results you seek? Because overseas lenders seeking to break into a new area:

- Market business and real-estate loans more aggressively
- Are willing to take bigger risks
- Have an open mind and yearn for unusual business deals
- Will often lower their interest rates to compete with local lenders.

You don't have to send letters overseas to deal with such lenders. Many of them have local branch offices in large cities. So you can contact them directly—by phone or mail. This saves you lots of time and reduces your phone and postage bills.

To get good results with overseas lenders, take these easy steps:

- Submit a short business plan with your loan application.
- Use the lender's loan app—don't try to substitute another lender's app; overseas lenders like their own app much better than those of others.
- Borrow for new, clean, expanding-market businesses—these have greater appeal to overseas lenders.

You can get a list of overseas lenders free as a two-year subscriber ($48) to the *IWS* newsletter. This list is updated regularly. So the names, addresses, and telephone numbers you get are right up to date. This is important.

New York city alone has over 400 foreign lenders with branches of offices in it. Chicago, San Francisco, and other large cities have as many as 100 offices or branches in each city. So the overseas lenders *are* there. All you need do is get in touch with them. That's easy!

Credit Unions Can Give You the Money Results You Seek

There are some 20,000 federally chartered credit unions in the United States today. Add to this the 50,000 state chartered credit unions and you have some 70,000 lenders.

Today a number of credit unions make business and real-estate loans. And you can get some of these loans if you approach the proper credit union in the right way. To get a credit union business or real-estate loan:

1. *Find out* what credit unions are near you. Look them up in the "Yellow Pages" of your phone book.
2. *Contact each credit union* by phone or mail. Ask what the membership requirements are, and what types of loans the credit union makes.
3. *If you can join,* and the credit union makes the type of loan you seek, ask for a membership app. Fill out the app and send it in with any small initial membership deposit required. Then ask for a loan application.
4. *Type the loan app*—don't fill it out by hand—it doesn't make a good impression on loan officers. Send your application to the credit union.
5. *Get your loan*—the money *result* you seek. Then use the money for the stated purpose. Start to repay the loan as soon as you can!

Many of my readers get credit union loans. Some of these loans are as high as $750,000 for real estate. While such a loan might not impress you, I know of thousands of BWBs who would welcome a loan of this amount. Some would even jump for joy with a loan 1/3 this amount, or $250,000!

Use Asset-Based Lenders for Big-Money Results

Asset-based lenders are those organizations (banks, finance companies, factors, etc.) that advance money against a firm's assets. Typical assets that can support loans include accounts receivables (what the firm is owed for work it did), equipment, real estate, inventory, etc.

Today, commercial banks are probably the biggest asset-based lenders in the world. Since such banks understand business, asset-based loans are easier to get than any other type of business loan. That's why I urge you to use such loans in building your million-dollar fortune.

How can you get asset-based loans for yourself or a client? Here are the simple steps to take:

1. **Decide** what collateral is available to pledge for the loan. Do this by checking the firm's assets against the list above.
2. **Figure** the value of the assets. Do this by having someone in the firm who knows the numbers give you the value. If *you* own the firm, you'll know the numbers from your own dealings in the business.
3. **Locate** an asset-based lender. You can do this through the Small Business Loan Kit listed at the back of this book, or by looking in your telephone book "Yellow Pages" under "Loans."
4. **Contact** the lender to learn if the collateral you've picked is acceptable. If it is, get an application from the lender and fill it out.
5. **Send** your loan application to the lender and wait for a response. If you have suitable collateral, the answer you'll get will almost certainly be a positive and happy *yes*. Why do we use these words in connection with the *yes*? Because asset-based lenders are—in general—so hungry for new business that they'll almost hound you for it. How do I know? I know from what they tell me during my monthly lunches with them in different parts of the country.

As some of my readers know, I'm President and Chairman of a major lending organization in New York City. At this writing we're pleading with our depositors to borrow more from us. Why?

Because any lender makes its largest income from the interest on loans. But if you're cash heavy and highly liquid as we are, you're not making as much as you should if you don't get your excess funds out on loan. So we scratch around—every day—to find new borrowers.

Asset-based lenders are in the same boat as we are. They're looking for borrowers day and night—everywhere. Why don't *you* help them put some of their excess cash to work earning your million-dollar fortune?

In my many telephone calls from other lenders, there are a number of asset-based funders. They call and say:

- Do you have any hot prospects for us?
- When will you send us some new business?
- We thought you'd send us 10 new prospects. You've sent us only 7. Where are the other 3?

All these calls lead me to think that these lenders *are* hungry for new business. Wouldn't you think the same? If you do—and I think you should—go out and help them get money into the hands of people needing it! Right *now*. Then you'll get the results you seek—a million-dollar fortune.

Remember—your mind can make you rich. If you approach business from a different and unique angle, you're almost sure to get positive results. Like a businessperson I know of who combines the best of new technology to build more sales. Here's what this business person does:

> Having a personal computer and FAX machine in his firm, this businessman decided to use them to send a direct response letter to 10,000 firms to sell business products. The computer produces the letter, which is sent out 60 times an hour by the FAX machine. The response rate was a spectacular 12% for orders averaging $2,000 each! So his marketing brilliance produced about $0.12 \times 10,000 \times \$2,000 = \$2,400,00$ in revenue. Not bad for one good idea to combine the best of the new technologies.

In using asset-based lenders you'll be using new ideas in lending. That's why your chances for success with it are high.

Why wait? It can be *your* Breakout Method for financing your way to your million-dollar fortune using your mind to make yourself rich.

Form an Offshore Bank to Attract Capital

You can form a bank in the United States if you have at least $1 million in capital. Most of the BWBs I know don't have money to form such a bank. And I think that most of my readers are in the same condition—somewhat cash-short at the moment.

But you can form a completely legal offshore bank for about $20,000. And this bank can do everything a domestic bank does, namely:

- Accept deposits
- Make loans
- Issue Certificates of Deposit
- Accept credit-card charges
- Work with other banks on deals
- Issue and handle Letters of Credit
- Make compensating-balance loans
- Serve corporate checking and savings accounts
- Become a member of various banking organizations
- Etc.

Some people open an offshore bank to get privacy for their financial dealings. To me this is really silly. Privacy doesn't increase profits. And profit—after all—is what will build your million-dollar fortune. So don't occupy your mind with privacy. Instead, seek profits—they'll build your fortune faster than any secrets will!

Offshore banks are usually located in remote areas needing new banks to build their economy. So when you form an offshore bank you help both yourself and others. To form your offshore bank:

1. **Decide** where you'd like to locate. When deciding on your location, remember that wire transfers, satellite communication, and overnight courier services make almost any location "just around the corner."

2. **Contact** the banking authority in the location you've chosen. Ask for copies of their banking regulations. These will usually be supplied free to you.

3. **Read** the banking regulations carefully. Try to understand all that you read. If there are words you don't understand, look them up in a financial dictionary.

4. **Consult** an attorney familiar with banking law. Ask the attorney if it is possible for you to form an offshore bank while complying with the regulations in the location you've chosen. If the attorney gives you the go-ahead, have the needed papers filled out by your attorney. (Don't do the final filling out. You can take a pass at a rough filling out—that's all.)

5. **Submit** the papers through your attorney. Pay any needed fees when you send in the papers. Then wait for approval. It may take weeks before you get your approval. But the wait could be worth it—if you run your bank to make a profit for you and any associates you may have.

Having your own bank is another Breakout Method that can help you build your million-dollar fortune. Sure, it *does* take some work and some cash. But the results are worth every moment of effort.

And by the way—the $20,000 fee mentioned above is for a fully first-class facility. This means the best of attorneys, full handling of all paperwork, and complete payment of any of the nominal fees charged by the government in the location where you want your offshore bank. You'll get the best results by using such an approach.

Results Are the Name of Your Efforts

I want *you* to be rich—to have a million-dollar fortune, or better. That's the *result* I seek for *you*. If you work for that result, I can almost guarantee that you'll reach your goal. How can I say this?

I can say it because I see hundreds of BWBs build a million-dollar fortune every year—using their mind to make themselves rich. Since these BWBs are not much different from you, I'm certain *you* can do the same.

And I'm here (in my office) to help *you*—day and night. Call me or write me—I'll try to help. It's a little easier for me to talk to you on the phone since when I write you a letter I'm not writing a book. So writing letters cuts my book-writing output.

But if you don't like to talk on the phone (some people don't), then drop me a line. Best of all, subscribe to my monthly newsletter, *International Wealth Success*, and you'll get a monthly "dose" of results-getting tips from me and from BWBs who're on the way to their million-dollar fortune using their mind to make themselves rich!

DAY 9

Owning your own successful business puts you in an ideal position. Why? Because you're ready to build on your early successes and acquire more wealth. Today you'll discover the methods you can use to build greater wealth in businesses that are fun to run and a gold mine for you.

CHAPTER 9

BUILD ON YOUR EARLY SUCCESSES—AND ACQUIRE MORE WEALTH

EARLY SUCCESS LEADS to more success—and wealth. Your mind can—and will—make you rich. All you need do is follow the tips we give you here. And keep pushing—every day of the week!

Studies show that 25% of people who are successful in a business branch out into a second business within two years after starting the first. And 66% are into a second business within five years of starting (or taking over) their first business.

So all the experience points to your being in more than one business five years from now! And—good friend—there's nothing nicer than having two sources of income. Except—possibly—having *three* sources!

With two, or more, income sources, when one is down the other will probably be up. So you have a steady flow of spendable cash into your bank every day you work! It's the greatest feeling of freedom you'll ever have.

Steady Progress Will Make You Rich

Once you get the skills needed to run a business successfully, you can transfer them to any business. In my own business activities I went from:

- Book writing to
- Billiard room ownership to
- Boating product sales to
- Newsletter publishing to
- Business and real-estate lending to
- Book and course publishing to
- Making grants for business to
- Consulting for business people and BWBs

And all these activities continue, earning money day after day. You can do much the same—in the businesses *you* pick for yourself. The income you earn will allow you to get the things you want most in life. Or it will allow you to get away from things you don't want!

To pick your next success, after your first success, take these easy simple steps:

1. **Decide** what new business you would enjoy. Do this by facing up to yourself and asking what you really enjoy doing. Use your mind to find what money-making activities turn you on. Why? They're the ones that will make you the most money!

2. **See how** you can branch out from your present business to the new business you like. There are a number of ways to do this. You can make the new business a part of your current one; or you can set up an entirely new business outside your current one. There's no one *right* way to do this. The choice depends on financing, the type of new business, etc. You must be the judge.

3. **Start your new business,** or take over a going business, as soon as you can after you make your choice. Don't delay—it only wastes time and someone else may come along with the same business. *Remember:* You always have an advantage when you're the first one with a new business in the area.

4. **Use your current business** to finance your second one. This will get you started faster. And you'll waste less time since you won't be trooping around trying to raise money. But if you enter a new business that has government financing available, apply for such help. Why? Because government financing is easier and faster to get than ever before. So you'd be foolish to neglect a good source of fast, low-cost financing. With the easy

availability of federal and state financing it is worth your time to check out all the opportunities open to you.

Popular Ways to Build on Early Success

Many of my newsletter readers take almost the same path to build on their early success. Here's a path that dozens of readers follow to build quick riches, using their mind to lead them to their million-dollar fortune:

- The BWB takes over some real estate with zero cash down. This real estate gives the BWB a positive cash flow every month.
- After operating the real estate awhile, the BWB sees that he or she has time on his or her hands. Why? Because real estate takes only a few hours a week to operate successfully. So the BWB starts thinking of the second business to enter to build more wealth.
- Many BWBs pick exporting as their second business. Why? Because, like real estate, exporting doesn't take much time. And the cash flow can be steady, week after week. Also, repeat orders can come to you automatically, without you even looking for them. Best of all, there's plenty of federal and state financing available for exports. With a firm order in hand, you're almost certain to get any financing you need.

Typical export financing from the federal government, or its agencies, includes:

Direct or intermediary loans up to $10 million from the Export-Import Bank at fixed or floating rates. Full information is available free from Export-Import Bank of the U.S., 811 Vermont Av NW, Washington, DC 20571. 202-566-8187.

Private capital for financing exports is available to overseas firms wanting to buy U.S. products or services. Full information is available free from Private Export Funding Corporation, 280 Park Av, New York NY 10017. 212-557-3100.

Leasing finance is available to overseas firms seeking to buy or lease U.S. products or services. Free information is available from Overseas Private Investment Corporation, 1615 M St NW, Washington DC 20527. 202-457-7105.

There are a number of other programs available for exporters. You can get the latest information on them by contacting the firms listed above. Also, the *Export-Import Kit* listed at the back of this book will give you much helpful information on financing exports.

And don't overlook your state business development company or agency. Plenty of money is available from such groups. If you want the name and phone number of your state business development group, just ask for it when you subscribe to the *International Wealth Success* newsletter for one year or longer. I'll be glad to send it to you at no charge.

From exporting, many BWBs move into financial brokerage. Why? Because the experience they get in obtaining financing for their exports has value to others. The BWB can sell his or her experience for a nice fee. And since neither the real estate nor exporting takes full time, there is time left over for financial brokerage!

So I see plenty of my readers entering this lucrative field. It's a "natural" because both real estate and exporting are "money businesses" in that they use funds to move ahead. So it's a simple step from finding money for real estate or exporting to raising money for others. This natural development brings the BWB *more* money, *more* experience, *more* confidence, and *more* growth—using his or her mind to make him or her rich. You can do the same—in fields *you* like. And I'm ready to help *you* start!

Join the Takeover Boom

If you don't want to start a new business, then take over a going business. You can do this using cash from your present business. Or—if you wish—you can try the zero-cash approach. In it you don't put down any money to take over the business.

Can you make money taking over a going business? You sure can, whether you pay for it with all cash, cash and notes, or just notes. For example:

A successful entrepreneur bought a famous hotel for $81 million. During the three years he owned the hotel it showed a profit of $12.5 million each year. He sold the hotel for $180 million about three years after buying it. The profit on the sale was about $150 million. This does not include the operating profit during the time the hotel was owned.

While I know you probably are not yet ready to invest $81 million in a business, this example does show you that:

- Profits *can* be made by taking over a going business.
- If run properly, the business will rise in value.
- You can sell the business when you have a buyer for it.
- Your profit on the sale can often run more than the operating profit while you held the business.
- Buying, holding, and selling a going business can be a big step toward your million-dollar fortune.

Dozens of my readers buy and sell businesses at a profit. You—I'm convinced—can do the same. If you do, you'll be joining the giant takeover wave sweeping the world. And you'll be making money from it—to build *your* million-dollar fortune. Let's see how you can get rich using your mind to build your wealth.

Three Ways to Get Rich from Takeovers

There are three good ways to make money from takeovers. You can probably come up with plenty of others. But here are three that work and work to make *big* money for BWBs:

1. Take over a company and run it for its profits.
2. Take over a company or property, fix it up, and sell it for a profit.
3. Take over a company or property, improve its profits, and sell it for more than you paid for it because of its higher profits.

find *VENTURE CAPITAL*
millions

Become an IWS VENTURE CAPITAL PROFESSIONAL and get the BIG benefits YOU can use NOW:

**Nearly instant CASH FLOW to YOU!
**Start a sizeable yearly income!
**Be in business quickly--NOW!
**Fast respect from others!

**Earn by mail, by phone, or by both!
**Get money for clients or yourself!
**Go from no-cash-flow to steady cash!
**Use the ONE-HOUR FINANCIAL WINNER!

Become an IWS VENTURE CAPITAL PROFESSIONAL and YOU get FOUR FAST WAYS to earn big!

**Be PAID to tell if a business idea is good!
**Be PAID to have a business plan written by others!
**Be PAID to find a venture capitalist to fund the deal!
**Be PAID for a piece of the success action--for years!

Get help ALL ALONG the way--while getting paid for getting others to do the work:

YOU get PAID while we evaluate the idea for YOU!
YOU get PAID while a business plan is written by others!
YOU get PAID while we find the venture capitalist for YOU!
YOU get PAID from future company growth--NO fees to us--ever!

GET IN ON THE BIG TIME NOW! How? By sending for the newest IWS Kit--THE VENTURE CAPITAL MILLIONS ONE-HOUR FINANCIAL WINNER! This breakthrough in venture-capital funding shows YOU how to:
°Raise venture funds fast
°Earn BIG fees sooner
°Get ongoing income for years
°Work where, and when, YOU want to
°Have others do the "nitty-gritty" for YOU
°Get started in just one hour, or less
°Be a professional, respected by all in your area
°Share in the newest deals in business and real estate
°Work without the need for a license of any kind

Anyone interested in money, business, or real estate can use THE VENTURE CAPITAL MILLIONS KIT! For someone just starting, it's the sure way to local "insider" deals of all kinds. And YOU can start in one hour, or less, if you want!

For brokers, finders, and business people it can be the source of NEW MONEY, much of which never has to be repaid! It can expand your world--go from small, puny deals to the BIG-TIME millions!

So send NOW for the Kit that could change your life! Or call IWS and put your order in by credit card. Be the first in YOUR area to offer venture capital professional services for any firm needing help from YOU!

Here's $100. Send me my VENTURE CAPITAL MILLIONS KIT. If you wish, YOU can call Ty Hicks at 516-766-5850 day or night to order by credit card. Or enter your card number below and send this coupon to IWS, Inc., 24 Canterbury Rd, Rockville Centre NY 11570.

NAME_____CARD NO._____

ADDRESS_____EXPIRES_____

CITY_____STATE_____ZIP_____

Buy this month and get Special Venture Capital List on self-adhesive labels updated every six months for one year!

Exhibit 9-1

Let's look at each of these ways and see how you can use it.

Take Over and Run for Profits

Let's say you like to ski. You spot a ski-equipment shop for sale. How? Where? In your local paper. Or in a national paper. Or listed by a business broker. What do you do? You take these steps:

1. You contact the owner and ask for details. The owner (or business broker) supplies these details. They are: income; expenses; profits.
2. You study the figures given you. They might look like those in Fig. 9-1. Since the store shows a nice profit, you get data on the asking price, cash-down asked, allowable payoff time if it isn't an all-cash deal.
3. You work over the price, cash-down, and payoff. If you don't have cash to put down on the business, then figure

Fig. 9-1   *Typical Store Income Statement.*

	Amount	*Percentage*
Gross sales	$300,000	100.00
Cost of goods sold	200,000	66.67
Gross profit	100,000	33.33
Other income	75,000	25.00
Total income	175,000	58.33
Variable expenses		
Payroll	80,000	26.67
Employee benefits	18,000	6.00
Supplies, equipment	1,200	0.40
Advertising and promotion	21,000	7.00
Utilities	3,000	1.00
Administrative and general	8,000	2.66
Total variable expense	131,200	43.73
Profit before rent	43,800	14.60
Rent	7,800	2.60
Profit before depreciation	36,000	12.00
Depreciation	3,000	1.00
Profit before income tax	33,000	11.00

out if you could borrow the money. Or decide if you want to try to get the seller to sell to you with zero cash down. This will mean that you'll have to negotiate. If you don't like wheeling and dealing, then forget trying to reduce or wipe out the asked-for down payment. Instead, try to borrow the money you need.

4. You work out *all* your loan payments to see that the business can make these while paying all its other bills, plus your salary. And you *must* be able to bank some money every month to handle any emergencies that might arise.

Only you can decide if the numbers are right for you. In buying a business on borrowed money you may have a lean period while the business repays the debts used to buy it. But once you pay off the debts you're in the money. Why? Because your former loan payments go directly into your pocket!

What is the key to taking over a business and running it for its profits? The key is:

> *The profits of the business must be large enough (or built up to a suitable level) so the business can pay for itself. Also, the profits of the business must be at such a level that after it pays for itself there will be enough income to make running the business worthwhile to you.*

When buying a business to run for its profits, be sure to look into yourself and know these aspects of your life:

- What you really enjoy doing in business
- Why you want to take time to make money
- Which business would be best for you
- Who might help you run your business
- When is the best time for you to take over a business.

If you don't know these aspects of your thinking, you may have trouble making as large an income as you seek. So get to know yourself. Your mind can make you rich!

Take Over; Fix Up; Sell

In this approach you will usually take over real estate of some kind. You will then fix it up. This you can do yourself if you're capable and like fix-ups. Or you can hire others to do the work for you.

In fixing up any property there are a number of cautions you should observe. These are:

1. **Get professional advice.** Don't try to fix up a property without the help of an architect who knows buildings of the type you're improving. The fee will be nominal and worth every penny!
2. **Get full approval from local authorities.** Don't go ahead with any work until the Building Department or other regulatory group approves your plans. If you go ahead with unauthorized work you may find that it has to be ripped out and done again. This will delay the eventual sale of the property and will probably raise the cost of the improvements.
3. **Borrow the money** for the improvement. You can pay off the loan when you sell the property. Meanwhile, you'll be building your million-dollar fortune using other people's money (OPM)—the best way to build wealth today.
4. **Get an appraisal of the property** before you put it up for sale. This way you'll avoid asking too low a price when you put the property up for sale. And get a real-estate broker to advise you on the best selling price for the property. Listen to what the broker says. Then decide what price you want to get for the property. Adjust your asking price upwards so you have some room to lower the price to what you really want for the property.
5. **Keep an eye on all contractors** working on your property. This will help you control costs better. And you'll make more money on the sale since you'll have invested less.

Fixing-up and selling takes a certain type of personality. If you don't enjoy working with your hands, or if you can't drive a nail straight, don't go into fixing-up. You'll be unhappy. Try another approach.

But if you're a good mechanic of some kind, consider fixing-up. Or if you enjoy working with your hands, try a small project first. You may find that you get great joy from the work. And I guarantee you this: You'll get more joy when you sell the fixed-up property at a profit!

Where do you find fix-ups? In your local and national papers, from local banks and mortgage companies, from the Veteran's Administration (VA), or from the Federal Housing Administration (FHA). You'll probably come across other sources if you get the word out that you're looking.

You'll find the VA and FHA (or HUD) listed in your local telephone book. Or you can write or call:

Veterans Administration
Washington DC 20420
202-293-2843

Department of Housing and Urban Development (HUD)
Washington DC 20410
202-755-6680.

Take Over; Raise Profits; Sell

Some companies or properties don't need a physical fix-up. Instead, they need new direction, new management, and new views to raise profits. Once the profits are higher, the firm or property will be worth more. Then it can be sold at a profit. To use this approach:

1. *Start looking* for firms or properties that are underperforming. Do this by checking your local paper, national papers, business brokers, and real-estate brokers. Check the *IWS* newsletter, also.
2. *Study the numbers* on those firms or properties you find. Determine why the company is underperforming. Typical reasons include lazy owners, absentee management, death of an owner, labor troubles, etc.
3. *Be sure you can cure* the ills of the business. If you're not sure you can, don't buy it! Why? Because if you're not certain you can improve profits of the business you're better off waiting until you find a deal that has promise for *you*. Stay away from trouble—it has a way of spreading. You can't build a million-dollar fortune if you have doubts about the first step you take on your way!
4. *Use good business methods* to control the profit growth of the firm or property you buy. Have an accountant and attorney nearby ready to advise you. The firm will

pay their fees at no cost to you. But you will benefit from their advice because the firm will sell for more when you're ready to sell it.

5. *Cut cost wherever you can.* One dollar saved in costs goes directly to your profit line. So every penny saved is a penny in extra profits for the business. Since the selling price of a business is based on its profits, the higher the profit you show, the larger the selling price you'll be able to command. With the higher selling price comes the larger profit for you!

Beyond all these guidelines, be sure to have fun building your million-dollar fortune in takeovers. Why? Because if you don't have fun making money you won't enjoy life as much. And your fortune won't come as quickly since you'll be straining to make big money.

Taking over a going business can cure any number of problems you might have. For those BWBs who would like a list of what owning your own business can do for *you*, here's a quick—and partial—rundown. Having a business can:

- Get you business loans under the firm's name that you might not be able to get under your own name
- Get you corporate credit cards that you can use for business expenses of many types
- Get you a line of credit in the name of the business that can give you greater money freedom
- Get you a nice office, warehouse, autos, trucks, airplane tickets, hotel accommodations, and meals for business use
- Get you out of debt by paying you a salary that you use to repay earlier debts you ran up
- Get you business cards, company stationery, telephone and FAX service for business use.

Now that you know a few of the advantages of having your own firm, aren't you ready to buy one? It could be the smartest move of your life. You can use your mind in your business to make yourself rich! As one reader recently told me:

My company is my life. It took me out of debt inside of a few weeks after it turned profitable—which was about three months after I started it. Then, when the profits began to pile up, I started to look around for something to do with the money. Before my eyes dozens of other companies and people with good ideas showed up. In just two weeks I bought three other firms with money from my first company. Today I'm worth about $5 million and I'm still growing. Not bad for someone who went bankrupt 5 years ago. By the way, the earnings from my companies allowed me to repay *all* the people I owed money to when I went bankrupt. So both they and I benefitted from my takeover activities. Thanks so much for your help and guidance.

Use Company Money to Raise More Money

There's no business as great as the money business! I've been in the money business for years and it has made me bundles. It can do the same for you. How can I be so sure? Because:

- I'm president and chairman of the board of a multimillion-dollar lending organization that's growing like crazy making loans to BWBs, and others.
- On the side I have my own lending organization, which has been making loans to BWBs of all types for more than 20 years. And—good friend of mine—every BWB has repaid every loan made to him or her.
- BWBs are raising millions every day using the guidance I provide them. For some it's very hard work. For others, the raising of money is an easy task. But no matter how much work it takes, the effort is worth the result—money in *your* pocket!

There are a number of ways for you to use money from your early success to raise more money. And none of these methods rely on borrowing! So there are no lengthy loan interviews, no scowling bankers looking over your business plan, no rejections. What are these ways to make money from your money? They are:

1. Form a Real Estate Investment Trust (REIT)
2. Form a venture-capital fund
3. Form a mutual fund.

Each of these ways of using your company money to raise money has similar features, namely:

- You need a "nest egg" to start.
- But your nest egg is never taken away from you.
- It stays with you but "greases the way" for millions of dollars you can command.

Let's take a look at each form of organization and see how you might use it to build *your* million-dollar fortune. You'll like what you see—I'm sure!

Real Estate Investment Trust

A Real Estate Investment Trust (REIT from now on) is an organization that raises money to invest in any type of real estate. And as long as 90% of its profits are paid out to investors in the trust, there are no federal income taxes on the trust.

REITs invest in all kinds of properties—office buildings, apartment houses, shopping centers, condos, etc. A "blind trust" is a REIT that does not tell its investors at the start what types of properties it will pick for investment. The REIT just states that it will aim for investments that will provide a profit.

While there is no set minimum money a REIT must have to start, you *do* need funds to get going. The actual amount will vary. But you should count on at least $10,000 in the REIT before you can start.

You can sell shares in your REIT yourself. But before trying to do this, be sure to check with an attorney who knows the law covering securities in your area. A share in a REIT is considered to be a security—just like a stock or a bond. So you *must* comply with the local and national securities laws. But this is really easy to do.

Let me give you the details of a REIT one of my readers recently took public himself. It shows you the kinds of business a REIT can enter, and the amount of money you might raise:

Shares issued: 10,000,000 @ $10 each = $100,000 raised.
Investment objectives: (1) Preserve investor's capital; (2)

provide quarterly cash distributions; (3) provide capital appreciation for investors.

REIT investments: Income-producing commercial and multiple-family residences; mortgage loans.

Expected leverage: As much as 80% for some properties (that is, 80% of the purchase price will be borrowed; the REIT will invest just 20% of the price); average leverage for all investments will not exceed 50%.

Types of investors: Individuals and other taxable entities (corporations, partnerships, etc.); qualified plans—IRAs, etc.

Now you don't have to seek $10 million for your REIT. You might need only $500,000. Or you might need $500 million. The choice is yours! Just be sure to take these easy steps:

1. Get competent legal advice every step of the way.
2. Be sure your REIT complies with all securities laws.
3. Find out if you're allowed to sell shares in the REIT yourself—you usually are.
4. Raise the needed money as quickly as you can.

REITs are the "way to go" if you want to build on your early success using real estate as your investment vehicle. So be sure to look into them if you want to build a million-dollar fortune.

Venture-Capital Fund

You can raise money for a venture-capital fund that will invest in new or growing companies. Your job will be to:

- ***Find*** new and promising firms in which to invest.
- ***Analyze*** each company and its future to determine if it's worth investing in and will give the desired growth.
- ***Decide*** how much to invest in the company, based on your estimate of its future growth potential.
- ***Take*** the needed investment action of advancing the money to the company.
- ***Watch*** the progress of the company by sitting on the board of directors yourself, or having one of your staff do this, making regular reports to you.

Almost all venture capital funds are sold to the public as limited partnerships. Each investor puts in $5,000, or more, per participation. Amounts you can raise run from a low of $500,000 to as high as $100 million. There is no legal restriction on the amount you can raise.

How can you successfully raise large blocks of money in a venture-capital fund? Here are methods that work well in today's market:

1. *Get a theme for your fund.* Thus, your theme might be technology companies, or medical-instrument firms, or aerospace products. The theme won't prevent you from investing in other types of companies. But it will give investors an idea of your general investing plans. If you pick a theme that's "hot," you may be able to raise millions in just hours. So choose your theme carefully. To do this, look around you today. See what's "turning people on." Try to relate your theme to one or more of these turn-ons.

2. *Pick a target amount to raise.* Don't settle for lesser amounts. Raise more than you think you really need. Why? Because your needs are almost certain to rise with time. Having extra cash on hand never made anyone poor! You can always invest it in safe, interest-earning accounts until you're ready to put it into a new and promising company.

3. *Aim at raising big chunks of money* at one time. How? By getting information on your fund out to pension plans, insurance companies, banks, brokerage houses, and others having large blocks of money seeking good investments. Using this approach will quicken your money raising and get you started in big-time venture capital sooner.

4. *Get local big names to help you* by serving on your board of directors. Their names will be an indirect endorsement of your fund and will make it easier to sell.

A venture-capital fund can be your way to a million-dollar fortune. The amount of cash needed to start such a fund can be as low as $10,000. But to be certain that you start right, be sure to consult a competent attorney, as suggested earlier. Then you'll be able to go from early successes to bigger ones—using your mind to make you rich. See Exhibit 9-1 for more data.

Form a Mutual Fund

You need $100,000 to form a mutual fund. Why? Because the law requires that a fund have that amount of money at the start. But note several facts about this starting capital:

- This money is never spent—it simply remains in the mutual fund as its basic capital. So the money is never lost.
- A successful fund can grow quickly, making the $100,000 look like "peanuts." So while the amount may seem like a lot at the start, it's just a drop in the bucket for a fund that catches on. For example, some funds raise $100 million in just a few months.
- You can invest the $100,000 starting capital in the same types of securities that you invest your shareholders money in. This gives you advantages in lowering investment fees, getting advice from experts, etc.

Again, as with a venture-capital fund, a mutual fund should have a theme. Without a theme you really can't market a mutual fund successfully. Some people will tell you that a good theme can almost guarantee that a mutual fund will raise $50 million, or more.

What are good themes. The best themes are those that tie in with current interests, market developments, world affairs, etc. Thus, there are themes covering:

- Industries—computers, electronics, space, etc.
- Countries—Japan, Korea, Germany, etc.
- Security types—bonds, growth stocks, etc.
- Real-estate opportunities—commercial, residential, etc.

Any other themes you can come up with could make you a fortune. Why? Because your input will be unique. It could generate millions in sales that other themes don't trigger. *Remember:* People often buy mutual funds on an emotional basis, instead of a clear, profit-making motive.

How do *you* make money from a mutual fund? You earn your money from fees your investors pay out of the money they invest in your fund. These fees can be:

- At the front-end—that is, taken out of the money investors send you to invest for them. Such fees are often 4%—that

is, $4 of every $100 goes to your mutual fund for expenses. If you wish, you can reduce the fee to, say, 1%.
- At the selling end—that is, taken out of the sales proceeds when the investor tells you to sell his or her shares in the mutual fund. This fee may be in the 1% range.
- For management expenses, taken out during the year. The total of such fees is usually under 1% of the total amount of money managed.

And you can set your fund up in either of two general ways—a *load* fund, or a *no-load* fund. In a load fund you charge front-end and management fees. The money you earn is the maximum that you can get in a mutual fund. In a no-load fund, there are no front-end fees—only an annual management fee. Here you may earn less than in a load fund.

The big key to keep in mind with any mutual fund is this: You *can* make big money from a mutual fund. And you're in a respected and honorable business. Any mutual fund provides you with an easy way to build on your early successes and acquire more wealth.

Become a Vacation Operator

Plenty of small business people complain every day—"I like this business and it gives me a good living. But I can't get away for even a day. My wife and I really need a long, long vacation. If I could only find someone to run the business for me for a week, a month—even a year!"

You could answer this BWBs "prayer." How? By agreeing to run the business for the time the owner wants off. You can—at almost *no* cost—make yourself a vacation operator. What you do is:

- Run a business while the owner is away
- Keeping help in the store or factory
- To run the business just as the owner would
- Making sales, delivering goods or services
- Depositing the cash and checks in the bank
- Keeping rough notes for the accountant
- And—above all—keeping the door open, the telephone answered, and the money flowing in—every day.

For such service any owner will be willing to pay you a very nice fee. Now you don't actually do the work in the store or the business. Instead, you hire people to do the work. But your current successful business allows you to:

- Sell the other owners on how efficient you are
- Convince doubters that you really know how to run any business
- Hire suitable people you (and the vacationing owner) can depend on
- Get more business as one owner tells another how reliable and dependable your service is.

The advantages to you of a vacation service business are great. Not only does such a business allow you to build on your early success to acquire more wealth, but it also:

- Gives you an inside peek into many other businesses
- Puts you in an ideal position to take over another business, as discussed earlier in this chapter
- Increases your income since you'll be paid a fee for your work
- Allows you to get rich on the efforts of your workers since all you have to do is assign them to the stores or factories where they'll work.

What kinds of businesses are good candidates for a vacation service? Not every business can use this type of service. But at least 80% of all businesses *are* good candidates. Typical of those worth thinking about for yourself are:

- Hardware stores, pet shops, gas stations
- Restaurants, motels, taverns, furniture stores
- Linen stores, electronic-equipment shops, ice cream parlors
- Travel agencies, dry-cleaning shop, quick-print store
- Video rental store, coin laundry, telephone-answering service
- Carpet-cleaning service, office cleaning service
- Employment agency, disco-nightclub, bicycle shop
- Women's clothing store, liquor/wine store, hobby shop
- Bookstore, muffler shop, parking lot, car wash
- Paint/wallpaper store, bridal shop, coffee shop
- Athletic equipment store, movie theatre, jewelry store
- Etc.

What kinds of businesses aren't suitable for vacation service? Here are a few. As you'll see, they are the types of businesses requiring a licensed professional of some type, such as:

- Accounting and tax practice
- Medical or dental practice
- Consulting engineering practice
- Legal practice of any kind.

Of course, if you're licensed as one of these professionals, you could offer them a vacation service, provided your skills are similar. Your professional ethics will guide you in this matter.

To form a vacation service for businesses, take these easy, quick steps to your expanded success:

1. ***Decide*** what type of business(es) you want to serve as a vacation specialist.
2. ***Get a list*** of such businesses in your area. You can start with the "Yellow Pages" and then move to local business directories available in your public library.
3. ***Write or call*** each business, telling the owner: "You can take a safe and profitable vacation! How? By using our Professional Vacation Service. You go; we work. We do all (or almost all) you can do—almost as well as you do!"
4. ***Line up workers*** who want just a few weeks work in the type(s) of business you'll serve. Fill them in on what they (and you) will do. Pay them a percentage (60% to 75%) of what you're paid. Be sure to impress on each worker the importance of quality and efficiency. Without these two features, your business won't render the type of service small business people seek.
5. ***Select your fee structure.*** Base your charges on what the traffic will bear in your area. To do this, you start with a typical manager's weekly salary. Scale this up to include an amount for your watching the manager. Then include an amount for your business profit. This last amount should include your inside overhead—rent, light, wages, advertising, management, etc. To see how this might work out, assume that the average manager's salary for your

area is $500 per week. Here's how you'll work towards your fee:

Salary of manager	=	$500.00 per week
Supervision of manager @ 10%	=	50.00 per week
Profit (includes inside overhead at 25% of manager salary)	=	125.00 per week
Total charge to client	=	$675.00 per week

This would be your fee for a small store. You might pay the manager you hire $300 per week. So your total profit will be $675 - $300 = $375 per week. All you do for this is see that the manager shows up and does a good job.

For larger businesses your fee, of course, will be much higher. Likewise, in heavily populated areas your fee will be higher because wages are—in general—higher in such areas.

Get Paid to Learn the Other Person's Business

The greatest advantage of this vacation service business is learning the ins and outs of the other person's business. While you can't learn everything about a business in two weeks—or even four weeks—you can learn much more than anyone might tell you. Thus, during your vacation service time you'll see:

- What typical income runs per day and week
- The kinds of problems the owner faces
- Which products or services sell the fastest
- The paying patterns of customers—cash, credit card, check, etc.
- Normal expenses the business faces.

While you're *not* spying on your client, you can't help but notice such items if you're an attentive businessperson. And a few days of supervising any on-the-spot manager will quickly tell you if you'd like to be in the type of business you're serving.

So while you're building on your early success to expand your wealth, you're also being paid to learn another person's business. Could anything be more fun and more profitable for *you?*

Use Zero Cash to Build on Early Success

Many BWBs think they have to take money from their first successful business to put into a second. Not so! You can use the credit power of your first business to float a loan to take over the second, third, fourth, etc. business. Let's see how this can work for you.

A successful BWB wanted to get a second business. But cash was tight. So here's how he took control of the second business—on zero cash. Using the credit power on his first successful business, he:

1. Got a bank loan for part of the down payment cash, using the credit power of his firm
2. Obtained an SBA (Small Business Administration) loan for the long-term mortgage on the business, again using the credit power of his first business, plus that of the second business
3. Got a purchase-money mortgage (a loan) from the seller to reduce the down payment cash
4. Took over what the seller owed various suppliers (the liabilities of the business) and used this as part of the total price since the seller was responsible for paying these bills, and then
5. Got the suppliers to extend the credit so the liabilities would not have to be paid off so soon.

All of these steps add up to the total price of the business, as you see in Fig. 9-2. The purchase price gives the BWB full control of the business and the sales it produces. And the profits of the business repay *all* loans besides giving you an income.

While your payments on these loans may seem "heavy," once the loans are repaid, you're in a highly profitable situation. You can then continue to run the business for its income, sell the business completely at a large gain, or bring

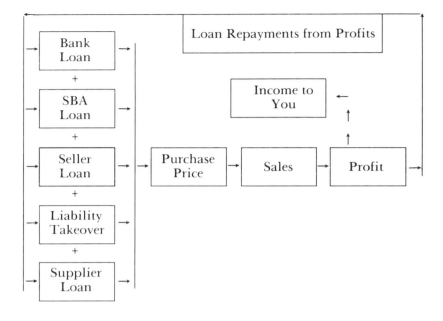

Fig. 9-2 *Financing a Business Purchase on Zero Cash.*

in a partner to run the business for you while you collect monthly, or weekly, profits for yourself.

Also remember that the interest paid on these various loans is fully deductible by the business on its income tax return. This deduction gives you a larger cash flow, helping you pay off the loans faster. Or you can use the money to pay yourself a higher salary!

Once you have a successful business it's easy to get into a second money-making deal. So why waste time and energy just "sitting" on one business when there are dozens of others seeking your skilled management? While you may be tempted to put up cash, it's better to go the zero-cash route because you'll have more money to enjoy the life you choose!

Million-dollar fortunes are made by people—like yourself—who want to have a business that makes them independent. The best way to "grow" such a business is to build on your early success. Then you'll acquire more wealth than you ever thought possible. Like this BWB who writes:

Last January I started full-time buying and selling residential real estate with the idea of holding some for rentals for the future. It has been successful far beyond my expectations.

During my first 5 months my financial statement shows I made $46,000. I averaged nearly $5,000 on every piece of property I sold. I have closed about 18 so far this year. (This would give a $90,000 profit for the year.) After nearly a year of experience, it's easier to buy good deals and I make more profit per house. Next year I expect to be able to handle 25 to 30 sales.

Another reader told me, on the telephone:

You know that I'm head of a religious group, being fully qualified by education and acceptance into the group I head. Three months ago, in order to branch out, I got the IWS *Venture Capital Millions Kit.* [See the back of this book.] Though I haven't made my millions yet, I *have* made $43,000 from deals I worked using info from the Kit. In just 3.5 months!

And I'm into much bigger deals, as a result of the first few. These include blind pools, meeting people with unlimited funds, and an $18-million construction deal. That Kit certainly has paid for itself—over and over—fast!

So you see, you *can* build on early successes. And I'm here to help—via phone or mail. You *can* acquire more wealth— starting today. All it takes is recognition of the fact that your mind *can* make you rich. Then, you *must* do something for your own good!

DAY 10

Once you're rich you'll want to share your success with others. Why? Because it's great fun, it makes you feel good, and—great news—it helps you prosper more! Here you'll see how you can share your success with others while helping them and prospering yourself! Could anything be more fun, more fulfilling, and more profitable to you? And to show you how we share our success with you, we're giving you four more days (10 + 4 = 14 days) to make up for any time you might have lost in building a million-dollar fortune using the 14-day success action program! Good luck—call your author (or write) if you need help.

CHAPTER 10

SHARE YOUR SUCCESS AND PROSPER RICHLY

YOU WILL BE A SUCCESS ! I'm so sure of this that I'm ready to help you in every way I can, with:

- Financing, if you need it
- Advice, if you'd like a "second opinion"
- Information you might need
- Guidelines for getting what you want.

These offers are part of my sharing *my* success with you—to help you prosper. At the same time I—too—prosper. How can I say this? I can say it because in helping thousands of BWBs I've noticed that:

- The more *I* help others, the richer *I* become
- Both in money and—more importantly—in friends
- While at the same time I have a great feeling of accomplishment—a feeling no money can buy
- And—at the same time—BWBs benefit too.

Spread Your Wealth to Help Others—and Yourself

My company—IWS, Inc.—has been in business 23 years at this writing. It has been very successful—using the methods given you in this book. We're so successful that we lend money to BWBs to help them get started or expand a business. The money we lend out is our corporate cash that we earned.

Beyond these BWB loans we lend our own money in another way. That way is:

- We buy the guaranteed portion (usually 90% of the loan amount) of SBA loans,
- Helping the bank that makes the loan get its cash back to loan out to others,
- While we earn a higher rate of interest and get monthly payments from the bank,
- With the loan fully insured by the full faith and credit of the United States Government,
- While we help the BWB who got the loan, the SBA, the bank, and the Government.

Everyone prospers because one company is willing to invest some of its cash in a government program that helps BWBs. By investing in the SBA guaranteed loan portion we're sharing our success. The BWB who received the SBA loan is better off; the bank has most of its cash back; and we feel good about sharing our success. (And—of course—we're receiving a higher rate of interest than we might on a money-market account, savings account, etc., while our money is fully insured.)

We even help BWBs get SBA loans sooner by agreeing in advance to buy the 90% guaranteed portion of the loan. If a BWB can say to a bank—"I have a buyer for your guaranteed portion of the loan," there's a much better chance for the BWB to get the loan sought.

As a reader of any of my books and my newsletter, I'll be glad to extend this courtesy to you. The top amount we'd consider putting into one guaranteed loan is $250,000. But sharing my company's wealth with you will help you prosper and help my company earn a higher rate of interest—fully insured!

How can *you* share your business wealth with others? There are a number of ways—all of which will help *you* prosper. Here are a few worth looking at:

1. Hire the people other firms overlook.
2. Sponsor community benefits.
3. Buy good equipment for your business.
4. Help banks get rid of repossessed properties.

5. Put excess funds into programs helping others.
6. Become a member of your industry associations.
7. Lend money to other businesses needing it.

Let's take a quick look at each of these ways of sharing your success. We'll see how you and your business can help others while you prosper yourself.

Hire People Other Firms Overlook

There are many competent people who—for one reason or another—most firms won't hire. These reasons include:

- Age—too young or too old
- Physical condition—lame, blind, etc.
- Race, color, creed, gender
- Etc.

You can help others while your business benefits if you hire certain of these people. Thus, we hire the elderly, the lame, the young, and minorities. And we find that these people are:

- Loyal—they never seem to quit.
- Hard-working—they work days, nights, weekends.
- Efficient—they get more done in an hour than anyone else.
- Helpful—they have many useful suggestions for us.

Women have put kids through college on the spare-time money they've earned from us. Some of our people have been with us for more than 20 years. And they rarely quit—in nearly 25 years only two people have quit. One left to go into her own wine-importing business. The other left because the travel distance from his home was too great.

So look around you. There may be many chances for you to hire people who'll be so grateful to you that they'll work for years and years. Better yet, check with your state Job Development Agency. You may find that:

- There are low-interest loans available to your firm
- For hiring disadvantaged or minority people
- Along with other benefits to your firm.

So while you're helping people, you're also gaining benefits for your firm. You might as well share your success if it helps *you* prosper more! Other benefits that might be offered by your Job Development Agency are listed in Chapter 5 of this book.

Get to know the people in *your* Job Development Agency. Why? Because they can do many other good deeds for you. Such as:

- Put you in touch with large firms making grants in your area.
- Introduce you to private lenders of many types.
- Get needed approvals of licenses quickly and easily.
- Publicize your firm free of charge to other firms in the state.
- Send your catalogs overseas to exhibits—free of charge.
- Invite you to important meetings of businesspeople—free.
- Send you free newsletters and other important announcements.
- Help you if you ever have legal problems.

Thus, by helping a few people in your area you can open up enormous benefits for your firm. Your employees profit from their regular wages you pay them. And your firm reaps large rewards from the assistance your state (and even the federal government) offer. So start sharing your success now. Use your mind to figure out what to do. For—as I said a few times before—your mind can (and will) make you rich!

Sponsor Community Benefits

Many communities have benefit programs for juniors, seniors, handicapped, reading-impaired, etc. Your firm can help such programs for little money. The benefits you'll reap include:

- Recognition by local people that you're a "good" firm
- Free listing in various program publications
- Mentions in speeches by high officials
- Association with top executives in your area

- Recommendations from people and other companies as to your community spirit and generosity.

For anywhere from $100 to $1,000, you can get highly favorable publicity for your firm and its work. Your contribution can be in the form of a grant, a gift, or even a loan to help the community.

Don't look for a direct return for your contribution. Instead, look for inclusion with the "good people" in your community. You'll even find that customers come in saying "I saw you listed in the _____ Bulletin. So I thought I'd give you a try. I've never used your services before."

Being among the good people will reap many rewards for you and your firm. One of them will be a feeling of helping. Another will be increased business. Could you ask for anything more?

Buy Good Equipment for Your Business

Some people in business scratch along with outdated typewriters, ancient computers, groaning production machines, and antiquated mailing meters. This is really silly. Why? Because:

- Business equipment is fully deductible on your business tax return
- Either as a depreciation deduction or as a cost item
- Thereby reducing the income tax you pay
- While at the same time it increases the efficiency and profits of your business
- Keeping your workers happier because they feel "they're state-of-the-art people"
- And they turn out more saleable products—faster
- And you help the equipment seller to become more successful.

So get to know what's new in your business. Learn how the new technology—such as fiber optics, compact disks, VCRs, fuel cells, solar energy, data bases, and minicomputers—can help you share your success and prosper.

All my life I've felt that new, modern equipment for business is essential. So I buy the newest for my business. And do you know what? My business booms—year after year. Better yet:

- People come to me and suggest new ways to earn more
- Giving me ideas they picked up from other businesses
- Helping me grow by insider's news and tips.

The same will happen to you if you buy good, new equipment. Stay away from used equipment. It's often more of a headache than you want. New equipment is a joy to use. And it's always covered by a warranty at the start. So there's no worry about breakdowns or failures.

Successful small firms I work with are more modern than some larger firms. These small firms:

- Use satellite transmission to send information to Europe where it's processed the same day it's received
- Then the processed data is sent back via satellite to local computers
- Which print letters that are sent to customers
- Or transmitted by FAX directly into a customer's office.

You, too, can use these, and other, methods to improve the efficiency of your business. You share your success by buying the other person's product and prospering with it! You use your mind to make yourself rich!

Help Banks Get Rid of Repossessed Properties

When a bank takes back a building of any kind (repossesses it) because the owner has fallen behind in payments, it has just one thought in mind:

- Get rid of the property to another owner
- Who will make regular, timely monthly payments to the bank
- Without causing a hassle of any kind

You can help banks with their problem properties (called Real-Estate Owned = REO) by:

- Using your company funds to search out the banks
- Via telephone calls and letters
- Then inspecting the properties that interest you
- And taking over those that have potential for you.

Thus, you're paying people (or yourself) to spend time deciding if the properties available are right for you. So you're sharing your success to help the banks while your firm prospers from the real estate it takes over.

And you will benefit in a number of positive ways. These ways include:

- An income from the real estate you take over
- A rise in value of the real estate you take over
- A profit on the sale of the real estate when you sell it.

A good friend of mine handles REOs in another way. You might be interested in doing what he does because it can make you a lot of money while you share your success. Here's what he does:

1. **Contacts** banks by phone and asks them for details on their best REOs
2. **Calls** real-estate brokers in the area of the REOs and tells them he has choice REO listings for them
3. **Charges** the real-estate broker for each listing he provides. While this charge can vary, a typical amount is $350 for one listing
4. **Gets** the real-estate broker to agree to pay him 25% of the commission on the sale of the property
5. **"Sells"** to real-estate brokers as many as 10 properties a day. That's a gross income of 10 × $350 = $3,500 per day—not bad for a day's work!

Of course, you must work hard at this business—finding banks and real-estate brokers who are interested. But the profits *are* there for anyone who wants to share success and prosper richly. All you need do is search out—with your mind—the opportunities open to you if you use:

- Modern technology to bring wealth your way
- By combining ideas for making money with good communications
- Provided by the computer, telephone, FAX, etc.

Put Excess Funds into Programs Helping Others

As we noted earlier, there are many ways for you to help others in business. But you can extend your help beyond just other businesses. For example, your firm can:

- Buy, and hold, municipal bonds for projects in your state, thereby helping build schools, roads, waterworks, bridges, highways, public transit systems, etc.
- Buy, and hold, U.S. Government bonds of various types, thereby helping the Treasury, Maritime Administration, Small Business Administration, etc.
- Buy, and hold, stocks or bonds of major corporations doing useful work for others. This way you inject cash into firms that get things done for people.

If you put excess funds into carefully selected investments you stand to gain in several ways, namely:

1. You will have a regular income from the investment. This income can be in the form of interest, dividends, and—possibly—special distributions.
2. Carefully picked investments will often rise in value. So you can sell—for a profit—some, or all, of your holdings.
3. There's a great satisfaction in having your business help other businesses, or the government. You recognize that there's more to success than just piling up money. But— as my accountant says—it's a lot of fun to watch the money pile up!
4. Your firm—no matter how small—joins "the big guys" when it invests in the large organizations offering stocks or bonds for sale. And—good friend—you'll learn more about business when you follow such a firm's activities. Further, when your money is invested you have a much more interested view than when you're just reading about a company in the newspaper.

Become a Member of Your Industry Associations

Almost every industry has one or more "trade" associations serving it. These trade associations do much useful work, such as:

- Obtaining and distributing financial data on the business
- Holding educational and information meetings for members
- Publishing and distributing data on the industry
- Helping you meet others in the business to exchange info.

So you gain in many ways by joining the key industry associations. For example, my company, International Wealth Success, Inc. (known for short as IWS, Inc.) is a member of:

- The Newsletter Association—this association, headquartered in Washington, D.C., is an excellent source of information on the newsletter business. It has a twice-monthly newsletter that's full of info on newsletter publishing and profits.
- The American Booksellers Association—this association, headquartered in New York City, has an excellent monthly magazine on bookselling. Its annual ABA Meeting is known around the world as "the place to be" to get the latest info on the newest books. And through its meetings we meet many other booksellers and exchange useful data.
- The Better Business Bureau, Long Island Section. I've already mentioned the many benefits of being a member of this excellent organization. You should join it and support ethical business practices for all your customers.

To me, the greatest benefit of trade associations is the people I meet at official (and unofficial) gatherings. For example, one person I met at a gathering said to me:

- "We ought to prepare an information kit on being an International Finance Consultant. What do you think?"
- "It's a great idea," I replied. "What do you think it should cover?"
- My friend thereupon told me what it should cover—topics such as:
    International sources of loans into the multi-millions
    Loan guarantees in the form of letters of credit, bonds, promissory notes, etc.
    Services for borrowers seeking business loans, venture capital, real-estate financing, working capital, lines of credit, import-export financing, etc.
    Plus many more

- The idea "grabbed me" and I agreed to help prepare more than half the kit while my friend agreed to do the advertising and promotion of the kit.
- Today we have a highly successful kit that's selling all over the world. We're both very happy with it. So happy that we're developing a second kit. This will be on international banking. It, and the *International Financial Consultant Kit,* are described at the back of this book.

You can join—through your firm—your industry association. The dues are tax-deductible. And I'm sure you'll help others as you share your success and prosper richly—using your mind to make yourself rich!

Lend Money to Other Businesses Needing It

If you follow my ideas on building wealth, you'll probably wind up with big, big problems. These problems? They are:

1. How, and where, to invest the enormous amount of money flooding into your business
2. What to do with excess cash you can't spend sensibly since you have all the things you want—autos, boats, homes, etc.
3. How to share your success to help others while still prospering yourself.

My answer to these "problems" is to seek to help others with their business difficulties. Studying typical BWBs throughout the world, the one problem they all seemed to share was:

- A lack of money for their business. The cash shortage took many different forms, such as the following. See if one, or more, describe your situation—or that of a friend or family member; these people need money for:
     Real-estate income property down payment
     Cash to buy a franchised business
     Down payment to buy an existing business
     Expansion capital for machinery, equipment, etc.
     Starting capital for a new business
     Accounts receivable financing

Working capital loan
Import-Export financing
Bridge loan for real estate or business purchase
Inventory financing
Revolving loan for any business or real-estate use
Operating loan to pay salaries or insurance
Monthly expense loan to pay rent or advertising costs
Loan to buy goods at a long discount
Business debt-consolidation loan
Clean-up loan to repay existing loans
Unsecured loan for any business use
Installment loan for business purposes
Line of credit for business or real estate
Secured loan for business or real estate
Leasing funding to obtain needed equipment
Fixed-asset financing of equipment
Time-sales financing
Factoring on a nonrecourse basis
Boat, aircraft, auto, and other vehicle loans
Etc.

* Besides a lack of money, these BWBs seemed to have big problems getting loans of the types listed above.

My answer to these problems? When we incorporated our business, about a year after it started, I asked our attorney to be sure to write into the corporate charter the right to make loans for business or income real-estate use.

You *can* make loans to other companies for business or income real estate use without being a "bank." A bank—remember—*accepts deposits.* If your firm makes loans but does *not* accept deposits, then it's not a bank!

But you *must* have an attorney write your corporate charter. Don't try to write the final version yourself! You can write a rough draft to show your attorney what you're trying to say. But the final version you submit (through your attorney) to the state *must* be written by the attorney. To give you an example of an attorney-written charter covering these lending rights, here's one. Read it carefully. But have your version written by your attorney; note that this is only a small portion of the overall charter:

For its purposes, on any terms and without limit, to borrow or receive money, and, from time to time, to make, accept, endorse, execute and issue bonds, debentures, promissory notes, drafts, bills of exchange and other obligations of the corporation, and to secure the payment of any such obligations by mortgage, pledge, deed, indenture, agreement or other instruments of trust, or by other lien, upon, assignment of or agreement in regard to all or any part of the property rights or privileges of the corporation wherever situated, whether now owned or hereafter to be acquired.

With approval by the state, we began making business and income real-estate loans throughout the country, and the world. To avoid running into problems we developed the following guidelines:

- No points, fees, retainers, or any other charges
- Other than the low interest rate of 6%—a rate acceptable everywhere as not excessive
- Repayment in one day to 7 years, at the borrower's choice, with or without principal
- Interest-only payments monthly until the final month when interest and principal must be repaid.
- Collateral of some kind required on every loan
- Loans only for *active* business or real-estate use.

To date we have made loans throughout the United States and in many countries of the world. Everyone has repaid us—in full!

So the sharing of our success has helped many other businesspeople. And at the same time we have prospered. Why? Because the interest we earn goes directly to our bottom—or profit—line. This means our profits rise since we now charge 12% interest, except on business emergency loans.

Why did we raise our rates? Because so many idiots refused to believe we were making 6% loans. So we doubled the rates and the idiots believed! People are really strange.

You, too, can go into the lending business to share your success with others. But before you do, consult your attorney to determine:

- If your corporate (or partnership) charter allows you to make loans
- What maximum interest rate you can charge
- Whether additional approval of any kind is needed
- Which types of loans you can make

In most areas, small personal loans are surrounded with intricate laws. So your attorney will probably advise you to steer clear of such loans. But business and income real-estate (again, a *business*) loans have few rules to conform to in your lending. Why?

Because most states believe that the businessperson has enough know-how and skill to avoid being misled. So, few rules are needed to protect the business from sharp practices.

Keep These Rules in Mind When You Lend

Lending money for business use is fun and profitable. But there are certain rules you should keep in mind. Based on 21 years of lending to small businesses, I suggest that you remember—at all times—that:

1. Money is a strange commodity. People tend to forget where a loan came from. So getting your money back often becomes a game. I suggest you avoid this type of game at *all* times.
2. Insist on getting valuable collateral on *every* loan. Not only does the collateral protect you in the event the borrower defaults. It also "shakes the borrower up," making him or her realize this is a serious matter and that the money must be repaid or the collateral will be lost.
3. Check out *every* borrower carefully. Don't be "taken" by any sad story of trouble, sickness, disloyal business partners, etc. See the situation as it is. Be certain the borrower's story is true. Some borrowers have very active imaginations and can dream up the best stories you've ever heard. Believe what *you* see—only!
4. Be certain the borrower has the ability and willingness to repay the loan—on time. You don't want to waste your time chasing a borrower. So examine the borrower's

income and financial statements very carefully! Don't—
as a general rule—lend when the borrower's payments
exceed 42% of his or her net monthly income.

5. Get to know your borrower *before* you make a loan. It's
not necessary that you meet a borrower face to face. But
get to know your borrower either on paper or over the
phone. Do this by talking to the borrower a number of
times, or by receiving several letters from the borrower
before you make the loan.

6. Always think: What will we do if the borrower does not
repay? List what you *will* do if the borrower fails to repay.
Prepare this list *before* you make the loan. And be sure
that every step in your list *is* possible to make and can
get you your money back. After all, this is the entire idea
of lending—to get your money back, with suitable interest
earnings.

7. Insist that every borrower use your loan application—
not that from another lender. Why? Because you can
evaluate your own application much faster. And it's easier
to see if the applicant is qualified when you're familiar
with the application form. If you'd like to see the IWS,
Inc. loan application form, ask for it when you subscribe
to our newsletter for two years, or longer. See the back
of this book for more information.

Yes, lending your excess funds *can* help you share your
success while you prosper. But be sure that you have enough
to lend—before you offer to make loans. Then be certain your
attorney tells you it's all right to do so. Lastly, never make
a loan unless you're certain it will be repaid!

Become a Specialty Lender or Finder

If you don't want to share your success by making general
business and real-estate loans, consider becoming a specialty
lender. What do I mean by that? I mean that you:

- Offer loans for just one or two types of needs
- And become known as "the person to see for a _____
  loan" in your area, and nationwide
- Limiting your clients to those dealing in the type of business
  that appeals to you.

For example, there are five active church lenders I know of in the United States today. If you want to specialize in church loans (you'll meet the nicest people around!), then you should deal with these five lenders regularly. Two use 800 numbers so you can call them free of charge to get a quick answer.

Further—good friend—churches are happy to pay the usual interest rates and loan fees. So you can "star" as either a direct lender to churches or other religious organizations. Or you can be a finder for such loans.

As a direct lender you'll earn interest on the loan you make. As a church loan finder you'll earn the usual 5% fee on the first million dollars raised, 4% on the second, etc. Either way, you'll be sharing your success with others while you prosper.

If you'd like the names, phone numbers, and lending criteria of the five church leaders, I'll be glad to send them to you free of charge when you subscribe to my newsletter for two years or longer. Just ask for the list. See the back of this book for more data on the newsletter.

And I might add that specializing in church loans is a great way to get started! Why? Because most financial brokers and finders overlook churches and synagogues as excellent sources of loans or finder's fees.

You will rarely find a church or synagogue that won't repay its loan in full and on time. Many repay ahead of time. And their wealthy members will often pledge excellent collateral for the loan.

So even if you're not making direct loans, your job as a finder will be easier. Why? Because:

- The lender will have superb collateral.
- You can get almost all the cosigners needed
- Repayment can be guaranteed by weekly collections.
- The people borrowing are honest to start with—they're not trying to rip off a lender!

There are plenty of other special loans you can look at. These include the following, for which you might be either the direct lender, or a finder for loans for:

- Clothing stores of all types—men's, women's, children's, sports, etc.
- Restaurants of all types, or just special types, depending on the area in which you plan to lend or work
- Food stores—again specialized or general. Food is our most needed daily commodity. And financing of some type is almost always needed.
- Nightclubs, taverns, entertainment centers—shunned by many lenders—can be a big source of profit for you. With high profits in a short time, you can limit your, or your lender's, exposure by keeping the loan to just a few month's time. Then there's less risk all around.

There may be other businesses that interest you. For instance, you'll find the following specialties most lucrative— either as a direct lender or a finder:

- Marinas, yacht clubs, sailing schools, charter firms
- Medical free-standing centers (also called Walk-In-Medical Offices)
- Doctors, dentists, chiropodists, chiropractors, etc.
- Attorneys, accountants, professional engineers
- Etc.

Expand Your Services

Many professionals today—especially in the medical and dental fields—are seeing their income decrease. Why? Because:

- Many alternative services offer lower costs
- Medical and dental plans have fixed fees
- Medicare limits fees that can be charged.

To counter this falloff in income, many health professionals try to increase the number of patients they see. The reasoning is thus:

If I can see 10% more patients a day, I can raise my income by 10%, or more. So I've got to get more patients through the front door.

The trouble is, most health professionals don't know how to find more patients. You can help them do this, while also getting them loans for new office equipment and furnishings. Meanwhile, you can earn large fees from the health profesional. You do *not* split fees. Instead, you're paid a fee for helping the health professional find more patients.

How do you do this? In a number of ways. You can take these easy steps—right now:

1. Get the health professional's name in front of large numbers of people—such as in labor unions, religious organizations, lodges, companies, etc.
2. Tell these groups that they can get a free examination of some type by visiting the health professional's office. If care is needed, the health professional will offer it at a reduced fee to the person coming into the office as a result of the publicity you get.
3. Get the health professional to do a Question and Answer column in the paper serving large groups. The questions can come from the group, or they can be common questions people ask a dentist, an eye doctor, a foot doctor, etc. Suggest at the end of the Question and Answer column that if the person has more questions that he or she see Doctor _____ at the office.
4. Make direct loans to the health professional, or act as a finder for such loans. Health professionals are honorable and reliable people. So you can either make direct loans or find a lender for these people with great confidence. Our IWS lending program has been delighted with the results of loans to health professionals.

Now this *is* work! It isn't easy to get publicity for health professionals. But once you get the knack of it, you can go along from one health professional to another, increasing your income each time. Those who like your service will recommend you to their professional friends. And your business can soon increase.

But it does take work! So if you just want to sit back and have money fall from heaven, try a different business! And if you find any such business, be sure to call me first—free on my 800 number. I want to be the very first person to try such a business! Why? Because I need a bigger yacht for my ever-growing family.

Seriously, though, the *Professional Practice Builders Kit,* listed at the back of this book, will help you get started. And it gives you a way to get loans for these same health professionals, while you increase their patient flow. You'll be very popular with them—that I guarantee!

Sharing Your Success Is a Great Payoff

A reader called me the other day. Here's what he said:

> Ty, you're always doing things for other people. Does anyone ever do anything for you?" I thought about his question for a moment and replied:"No, Tom, not many people do anything for me. But I never asked that anyone do anything. Further, I don't expect anything from others. But I can tell you this—the joy of helping others is the best reward I could ever have. I'm so grateful to be able to help others that I never look for them to do something for me!"

Another reader called to say:

> I've read four of your books. They helped me a lot. For instance, I got loans I never thought I could get. And people who said it couldn't be done were astounded that I did what I did. In fact, I even astounded myself! Because there's always that little question: Is this guy (Ty Hicks) for *real*? I found you *are* for real and I'm ready to tell a lot of people that. Thanks so much for helping me with your ideas and motivation.

Yes, good friend, your mind *can* make you rich! But you must take the steps that lead to riches. I'm here to help *you* take those steps—starting right *now.* So you really have no one else to blame for a lack of wealth but yourself.

But time is passing. You must move ahead every day of the year—holidays included. Even if you do nothing but relax on a holiday to recharge your batteries for the next day, you're still making headway toward *your* riches.

Truly—good friend—you *can* build a million-dollar fortune—using your mind to make yourself rich. I'm so convinced of this fact that:

- I'm at the other end of your phone to help you—day or night
- I'll answer the letters you write asking for help
- My company's financial resources are at your service to help finance your business ideas.

So all I can say is that you can blame only yourself if you don't take advantage of my offer. Try me and see! I want to see *you* with the million dollars you built using the 14-day success action program. So be sure to write or call and tell me what you did!

BIBLIOGRAPHY

Other Profit-Building Tools from Tyler Hicks' *INTERNATIONAL WEALTH SUCCESS* Library

As the publisher of the famous *INTERNATIONAL WEALTH SUCCESS* newsletter, Ty Hicks has put together a remarkable library of dynamic books, each geared to help the opportunity-seeking individual—the kind of person who is ready and eager to achieve the financial freedom that comes from being a SUCCESSFUL entrepreneur. Financial experts agree that only those who own their own businesses or invest their money wisely can truly control their future wealth. And yet, far too many who start a business or an investment program of their own do not have the kind of information that can make the difference between success and failure.

Here, then, is a list of publications hand-picked by Ty Hicks, written especially to give you, the enterprising wealth builder, the critical edge that belongs solely to those who have the *inside* track. So take advantage of this unique opportunity to order this confidential information. (These books are *not* available in bookstores.) Choose the publications that can help you the most and send the coupon page with your remittance. Your order will be processed as quickly as possible to expedite your success. (Please note: If, when placing an order, you prefer not to cut out the coupon, simply photocopy the order page and send in the duplicate.)

IWS-1   ***BUSINESS CAPITAL SOURCES.*** Lists more than 1,500 lenders of various types—banks, insurance companies, commercial finance firms, factors, leasing firms, overseas lenders, venture-capital firms, mortgage companies, and others. $15. 150 pgs.

IWS-2   ***SMALL BUSINESS INVESTMENT COMPANY DIRECTORY AND HANDBOOK.*** Lists more than 400 small business investment companies that invest in small businesses to help them prosper. Also gives tips on financial management in business. $15. 135 pgs.

IWS-3   ***WORLDWIDE RICHES OPPORTUNITIES,*** Vol. 1. Lists more than 2,500 overseas firms seeking products to import. Gives name of product(s) sought, or service(s) sought, and other important data needed by exporters and importers. $25. 283 pgs.

IWS-4 **WORLDWIDE RICHES OPPORTUNITIES,** Vol. 2. Lists more than 2,500 overseas firms seeking products to import. (Does NOT duplicate Volume 1.) Lists loan sources for some exporters in England. $25. 223 pgs.

IWS-5 **HOW TO PREPARE AND PROCESS EXPORT-IMPORT DOCUMENTS.** Gives data and documents for exporters and importers, including licenses, declarations, free-trade zones abroad, bills of lading, custom duty rulings. $25. 170 pgs.

IWS-6 **SUPPLEMENT TO HOW TO BORROW YOUR WAY TO REAL ESTATE RICHES.** Using government sources compiled by Ty Hicks, lists numerous mortgage loans and guarantees, loan purposes, amounts, terms, financing charge, types of structures financed, loan-value ratio, special factors. $15. 87 pgs.

IWS-7 **THE RADICAL NEW ROAD TO WEALTH** by A. David Silver. Covers criteria for success, raising venture capital, steps in conceiving a new firm, the business plan, how much do you have to give up, economic justification. $15. 128 pgs.

IWS-8 **60-DAY FULLY FINANCED FORTUNE** is a short BUSINESS KIT covering what the business is, how it works, naming the business, interest amortization tables, state securities agencies, typical flyer used to advertise, typical applications. $29.50. 136 pgs.

IWS-9 **CREDITS AND COLLECTION BUSINESS KIT** is a 2-book kit covering fundamentals of credit, businesses using credits and collection methods, applications for credit, setting credit limit, Fair Credit Reporting Act, collection percentages, etc. Gives 10 small businesses in this field. $29.50. 147 pgs.

IWS-10 **MIDEAST AND NORTH AFRICAN BANKS AND FINANCIAL INSTITUTIONS.** Lists more than 350 such organizations. Gives name, address, telephone, and telex number for most. $15. 30 pgs.

IWS-11 **EXPORT MAIL-ORDER.** Covers deciding on products to export, finding suppliers, locating overseas firms seeking exports, form letters, listing of firms serving as export management companies, shipping orders, and more. $17.50. 50 pgs.

IWS-12 **PRODUCT EXPORT RICHES OPPORTUNITIES.** Lists over 1,500 firms offering products for export — includes agricultural, auto, aviation, electronic, computers, energy, food, healthcare, mining, printing, and robotics. $21.50. 219 pgs.

IWS-13   **DIRECTORY OF HIGH - DISCOUNT MERCHANDISE SOURCES.** Lists more than 1,000 sources of products with full name, address, and telephone number for items such as auto products, swings, stuffed toys, puzzles, oils and lubricants, CB radios, and belt buckles. $17.50. 97 pgs.

IWS-14   **HOW TO FINANCE REAL ESTATE INVESTMENTS** by Roger Johnson. Covers basics, the lending environment, value, maximum financing, rental unit groups, buying mobile-home parks, and conversions. $21.50. 265 pgs.

IWS-15   **DIRECTORY OF FREIGHT FORWARDERS AND CUSTOM HOUSE BROKERS.** Lists hundreds of these firms throughout the United States which help in the import/export business. $17.50. 106 pgs.

IWS-16   **CAN YOU AFFORD NOT TO BE A MILLIONAIRE?** by Marc Schlecter. Covers international trade, base of operations, stationery, worksheet, starting an overseas company, metric measures, profit structure. $10. 202 pgs.

IWS-17   **HOW TO FIND HIDDEN WEALTH IN LOCAL REAL ESTATE** by R. H. Jorgensen. Covers financial tips, self-education, how to analyze property for renovation, the successful renovator is a "cheapskate," property management, and getting the rents paid. $17.50. 133 pgs.

IWS-18   **HOW TO CREATE YOUR OWN REAL-ESTATE FORTUNE** by Jens Nielsen. Covers investment opportunities in real estate, leveraging, depreciation, remodeling your deal, buy- and lease-back, understanding your financing. $17.50. 117 pgs.

IWS-19   **REAL-ESTATE SECOND MORTGAGES** by Ty Hicks. Covers second mortgages, how a second mortgage finder works, naming the business, registering the firm, running ads, expanding the business, and limited partnerships. $17.50. 100 pgs.

IWS-20   **GUIDE TO BUSINESS AND REAL ESTATE LOAN SOURCES.** Lists hundreds of business and real-estate lenders, giving their lending data in very brief form. $25. 201 pgs.

IWS-21   **DIRECTORY OF 2,500 ACTIVE REAL-ESTATE LENDERS.** Lists 2,500 names and addresses of direct lenders or sources of information on possible lenders for real estate. $25. 197 pgs.

IWS-22   **IDEAS FOR FINDING BUSINESS AND REAL ESTATE CAPITAL TODAY.** Covers raising public money, real estate financing, borrowing methods, government loan sources, and venture money. $24.50. 62 pgs.

IWS-23   **HOW TO BECOME WEALTHY PUBLISHING A NEWSLETTER** by E. J. Mall. Covers who will want your newsletter, planning your newsletter, preparing the first issue, direct mail promotions, keeping the books, building your career. $17.50. 102 pgs.

IWS-24   **NATIONAL DIRECTORY OF MANUFACTURERS' REPRESENTATIVES.** Lists 5,000 mfrs.' reps. from all over the United States, both in alphabetical form and state by state; gives markets classifications by SIC. $28.80. 782 pgs., hardcover.

IWS-25   **BUSINESS PLAN KIT.** Shows how to prepare a business plan to raise money for any business. Gives several examples of successful business plans. $29.50. 150 pgs.

IWS-26   **MONEY RAISER'S DIRECTORY OF BANK CREDIT CARD PROGRAMS.** Shows the requirements of each bank listed for obtaining a credit card from the bank. Nearly 1000 card programs at 500 of the largest U.S. banks are listed. Gives income requirements, job history, specifications, etc. $19.95. 150 pgs.

IWS-27   **GLOBAL COSIGNERS AND MONEY FINDERS ASSOCIATION.** Publicize your need for a cosigner to get a business or real estate loan. Your need is advertised widely under a Code Number so your identity is kept confidential. $50.

IWS-28   **WALL STREET SYNDICATORS.** Lists 250 active brokerage houses who might take your company public. Gives numerous examples of actual, recent, new stock offerings of start-up companies. $15. 36 pgs.

IWS-29   **COMPREHENSIVE LOAN SOURCES FOR BUSINESS AND REAL ESTATE LOANS.** Gives hundreds of lenders' names and addresses and lending guidelines for business and real estate loans of many different types. $25; 136 pages. 8½ × 11 in.

IWS-30   **DIVERSIFIED LOAN SOURCES FOR BUSINESS AND REAL ESTATE LOANS.** Gives hundreds of lenders' names and addresses and lending guidelines for business and real estate loans of many different types. Does not duplicate IWS-29. $25; 136 pages; 8½ × 11 in.

IWS-31   **CREDIT POWER REPORTS**—five helpful reports to improve your credit rating and credit line. Report No. 1: *How to Get a Visa and/or Mastercard Credit Card*; $19.95; 192 pages; 5 × 8 in. Report No. 2: *How to Increase Your Credit Limits, Plus Sophisticated Credit Power Strategies*; $19.95; 208 pages; 5 × 8 in. Report No. 3: *How to Repair Your Credit*; $19.95; 256 pages; 5 × 8 in. Report No. 4: *How to Reduce Your Monthly Payments*; $19.95; 192 pages; 5 × 8 in. Report No. 5: *How to Wipe Out Your Debts Without Bankruptcy*; $19.95; 152 pages. Each book is also available on a cassette tape which duplicates the entire content of the report. The tapes are priced at $19.95 each and run 60 minutes. Please specify which tape you want when ordering; the tape title duplciates the report title.

IWS-32 **GUARANTEED MONTHLY INCOME** gives you a way to earn money every month via mail order selling books and kits to people seeking a business of their own. With this plan the money comes to you and you keep a large share of it for yourself. $15; 36 pages; 8½ × 11 in.

Newsletters

IWSN-1 **INTERNATIONAL WEALTH SUCCESS,** Ty Hicks' monthly newsletter published 12 times a year. This 16-page newsletter covers loan and grant sources, real-estate opportunities, business opportunities, import-export, mail order, and a variety of other topics on making money in your own business. Every subscriber can run one free classified advertisement of 40 words, or less, each month, covering business or real-estate needs or opportunities. The newsletter has a worldwide circulation, giving readers and advertisers very broad coverage. Started in Jan., 1967, the newsletter has been published continuously since that date. $24.00 per year; 16 pages plus additional inserts; 8½ × 11 in.; monthly.

IWSN-2 **MONEY WATCH BULLETIN,** a monthly coverage of 100 or more active lenders for real estate and business purposes. The newsletter gives the lender's name, address, telephone number, lending guidelines, loan ranges, and other helplful information. All lender names were obtained within the last week; the data is therefore right up to date. Lender's names and addresses are also provided on self-stick labels on an occasional basis. Also covers venture capital and grants. $95.00; 20 pages; 8½ × 11 in.; monthly; 12 times per year.

Success Kits

K-1 **FINANCIAL BROKER/FINDER/BUSINESS BROKER/CONSULTANT SUCCESS KIT** shows YOU how to start your PRIVATE business as a Financial Broker/Finder/Business Broker/Consultant! As a Financial Broker YOU find money for firms seeking capital and YOU are paid a fee. As a Finder YOU are paid a fee for finding things (real estate, raw materials, money, etc.) for people and firms. As a Business Broker YOU help in the buying or selling of a business—again for a fee. See how to collect BIG fees. Kit includes typical agreements YOU can use, plus 4 colorful membership cards (each 8 × 10 in.). Only $99.50. 12 Speed-Read books, 485 pgs., 8½ × 11 in., 4 membership cards.

K-2 **STARTING MILLIONAIRE SUCCESS KIT** shows YOU how to get started in a number of businesses which might make YOU a millionaire sooner than YOU think! Businesses covered in this big kit include Mail Order, Real Estate, Export/Import, Limited Partnerships, etc. This big kit includes 4 colorful membership cards (each 8 × 10 in.). These are NOT the same ones as in the Financial Broker kit. So ORDER your STARTING MILLIONAIRE KIT now—only $99.50. 12 Speed-Read books, 361 pgs., 8½ × 11 in., 4 membership cards.

K-3 **FRANCHISE RICHES SUCCESS KIT** is the only one of its kind in the world (we believe). What this big kit does is show YOU how to collect BIG franchise fees for YOUR business ideas which can help others make money! So instead of paying to use ideas, people PAY YOU to use YOUR ideas! Franchising is one of the biggest businesses in the world today. Why don't YOU get in on the BILLIONS of dollars being grossed in this business today? Send $99.50 for your FRANCHISE KIT now. 7 Speed-Read books, 876 pgs., 6 × 9 & 8½ × 11 in. & 5 × 8 in.

K-4 **MAIL ORDER RICHES SUCCESS KIT** shows YOU how YOU can make a million in mail order/direct mail, using the known and proven methods of the experts. This is a kit which is different (we think) from any other—and BETTER than any other! It gives YOU the experience of known experts who've made millions in their own mail order businesses, or who've shown others how to do that. This big kit also includes the Ty Hicks book "How I Grossed More Than One Million Dollars in Mail Order/Direct Mail Starting with NO CASH and Less Know-how." So send $99.50 TODAY for your MAIL ORDER SUCCESS KIT. 9 Speed-Read books, 927 pgs., 6 × 9 & 8½ × 11 in.

K-5 **ZERO CASH SUCCESS TECHNIQUES KIT** shows YOU how to get started in YOUR own going business or real estate venture with NO CASH! Sound impossible? It really IS possible—as thousands of folks have shown. This big kit, which includes a special book by Ty Hicks on "Zero Cash Takeovers of Business and Real Estate," also includes a 58-minute cassette tape by Ty on "Small Business Financing." On this tape, Ty talks to YOU! See how YOU can get started in YOUR own business without cash and with few credit checks. To get your ZERO CASH SUCCESS KIT, send $99.50 NOW. 7 Speed-Read books, 876 pgs., 8½ × 11 in. for most, 58-minute cassette tape.

K-6 ***REAL ESTATE RICHES SUCCESS KIT*** shows YOU how to make BIG money in real estate as an income property owner, a mortgage broker, mortgage banker, real estate investment trust operator, mortgage money broker, raw land speculator, and industrial property owner. This is a general kit, covering all these aspects of real estate, plus many, many more. Includes many financing sources for YOUR real estate fortune. But this big kit also covers how to buy real estate for the lowest price (down payments of NO CASH can sometimes be set up), and how to run YOUR real estate for biggest profits. Send $99.50 NOW for your REAL ESTATE SUCCESS KIT. 6 Speed-Read books, 466 pgs., 8½ × 11 in.

K-7 ***BUSINESS BORROWERS COMPLETE SUCCESS KIT*** shows YOU how and where to BORROW money for any business which interests YOU. See how to borrow money like the professionals do! Get YOUR loans faster, easier because YOU know YOUR way around the loan world! This big kit includes many practice forms so YOU can become an expert in preparing acceptable loan applications. Also includes hundreds of loan sources YOU might wish to check for YOUR loans. Send $99.50 NOW for your BUSINESS BORROWERS KIT. 7 Speed-Read books, 596 pgs., 8½ × 11 in.

K-8 ***RAISING MONEY FROM GRANTS AND OTHER SOURCES SUCCESS KIT*** shows YOU how to GET MONEY THAT DOES NOT HAVE TO BE REPAID if YOU do the task for which the money was advanced. This big kit shows YOU how and where to raise money for a skill YOU have which can help others live a better life. And, as an added feature, this big kit shows YOU how to make a fortune as a Fund Raiser—that great business in which YOU get paid for collecting money for others or for yourself! This kit shows YOU how you can collect money to fund deals YOU set up. To get your GRANTS KIT, send $99.50 NOW. 7 Speed-Read books, 496 pgs., 8½ × 11 in. for most.

K-9 ***FAST FINANCING OF YOUR REAL ESTATE FORTUNE SUC-CESS KIT*** shows YOU how to raise money for real estate deals. YOU can move ahead faster if YOU can finance your real estate quickly and easily. This is NOT the same kit as the R.E. RICHES KIT listed above. Instead, the FAST FINANCING KIT concentrates on GETTING THE MONEY YOU NEED for YOUR real estate deals. This big kit gives YOU more than 2,500 sources of real estate money all over the U.S. It also shows YOU how to find deals which return BIG income to YOU but are easier to finance than YOU might think! To get started in FAST FINANCING, send $99.50 today. 7 Speed-Read books, 523 pgs., 8½ × 11 in. for most.

K-10 **LOANS BY PHONE KIT** shows YOU how and where to get business, real estate, and personal loans by telephone. With just 32 words and 15 seconds of time YOU can determine if a lender is interested in the loan you seek for yourself or for someone who is your client — if you're working as a loan broker or finder. This kit gives you hundreds of telephone lenders. About half have 800 phone numbers, meaning that your call is free of long-distance charges. Necessary agreement forms are also included. This blockbuster kit has more than 150 pages. 8½ × 11 in. Send $100 *now* and get started in one hour.

K-11 **LOANS BY MAIL KIT** shows YOU how and where to get business, real estate, and personal loans for yourself and others by mail. Lists hundreds of lenders who loan by mail. No need to appear in person — just fill out the loan application and send it in by mail. Many of these lenders give unsecured signature loans to qualified applicants. Use this kit to get a loan by mail yourself. Or become a loan broker and use the kit to get started. Unsecured signature loans by mail can go as high as $50,000 and this kit lists such lenders. The kit has more than 150 pages. 8½ × 11 in. Send $100 *now* to get started in just a few minutes.

K-12 **REAL-ESTATE LOAN GETTERS SERVICE KIT** shows the user how to get real estate loans for either a client or the user. Lists hundreds of active real estate lenders seeking first and junior mortgage loans for a variety of property types. Loan amounts range from a few thousand dollars to many millions, depending on the property, its location, and value. Presents typical application and agreement forms for use in securing real estate loans. *No* license is required to obtain such loans for oneself or others. Kit contains more than 150 pages. 8½ × 11 in. Send $100 *now* to get started.

K-13 **CASH CREDIT RICHES SYSTEM KIT** shows the user three ways to make money from credit cards: (1) as a merchant account, (2) helping others get credit cards of their choice and (3) getting loans through lines of credit offered credit card holders. Some people handling merchant account orders report an income as high as $10,000 a day. While this kit does not, and will not, guarantee such an income level, it *does* show the user how to get started making money from credit cards easily and quickly. The kit has more than 150 pages. 8½ × 11 in. Send $100 *now* to get started soon.

K-14 ***PROFESSIONAL PRACTICE BUILDERS KIT*** shows YOU how to make up to $1,000 a week part time, over $5,000 a week full time, according to the author, Dr. Alan Weisman. What YOU do is show professionals — such as doctors, dentists, architects, accountants, lawyers — how to bring more clients into the office and thereby increase their income. Step-by-step procedure gets you started. Provides forms, sample letters, brochures, and flyers YOU can use to get an income flowing into your bank in less than one week. The kit has more than 150 8½ × 11 in. pages. Send $100 *now!* Start within just a few hours in your local area.

K-15 ***VENTURE CAPITAL MILLIONS KITS.*** Shows how to raise venture capital for yourself or for others. Gives steps for preparing an Executive Summary, business plan, etc. You can use the kit to earn large fees raising money for new or established firms. $100. 200 pgs.

K-16 ***GUARANTEED LOAN MONEY.*** Shows how to get loans of all types—unsecured signature, business, real estate, etc.—when your credit is not the strongest. Gives full directions on getting cosigners, comakers, and guarantors. $100. 250 pgs.

K-17 ***IMPORT-EXPORT RICHES KIT*** shows you how to get rich in import-export in today's product-hungry world. This big kit takes you from your first day in the business to great success. It gives you 5,000 products wanted by overseas firms, the name and address of each firm, procedures for preparing export-import documents, how to correspond in four different languages with complete sentences and letters, names and addresses of freight forwarders you can use, plus much more. Includes more than 6 books of over 1,000 pages of useful information. $99.50.

K-18 ***PHONE-IN/MAIL-IN GRANTS KIT.*** This concise kit shows the reader how to jump on the grants bandwagon and get small or large money grants quickly and easily. Gives typical grant proposals and shows how to write each so you win the grant you seek. Takes the reader by the hand and shows how to make telephone calls to grantors to find if they're interested in your grant request. You are given the actual words to use in your call and in your proposal. Also includes a list of foundations that might consider your grant application. $100; 200 pages, 8½ × 11 in.

K-19 ***MEGA MONEY METHODS*** covers the raising of large amounts of money—multimillions and up—for business and real-estate projects of all types. Shows how to prepare loan packages for very large loans, where to get financing for such loans, what fees to charge after the loan is obtained, plus much more. Using this kit, the BWB should be able to prepare effective loan requests for large amounts of money for suitable projects. The kit also gives the user a list of offshore lenders for big projects. $100; 200 pages; 8½ × 11 in.

K-20 **FORECLOSURES AND OTHER DISTRESSED PROPERTY SALES** shows how, and where to make money from foreclosures, trustee sales, IRS sales, bankruptcies, and sheriff sales of real estate. The kit contains six cassette tapes plus a workbook containing many of the forms you need in foreclosure and trustee sales. Addresses of various agencies handling such sales are also given. $51.95; 80 pages and 6 cassette tapes. 8½ × 11 in.

K-21 **SMALL BUSINESS LOAN PROGRAM** is designed to obtain loans for small and minority-owned businesses doing work for government agencies, large corporations, hospitals, universities, and similar organizations. The small business loan program pays up to 80% on accounts receivables within 48 hours to manufacturers, distributors, janitorial services, building contractors, etc. Startups acceptable. You earn a good commission getting these loans funded, and receive an ongoing payment when the company places future accounts receivable with the lender. $100; 200 pages; 8½ × 11 in.

K-22 **PHONE-IN MINI-LEASE PROGRAM** helps you earn commissions getting leases for a variety of business equipment—personal computers, copy machines, typewriters, laser printers, telephone systems, office furniture, satellite antennas, store fixtures, etc. You earn direct commissions of 3% to 10% of the cost of the equipment up to $10,000. You get immediate approval of the lease by phone and the lender finances the equipment for the company needing it. Your commission is paid by the lender directly to you. $100; 150 pages; 8½ × 11 in.

K-23 **INTERNATIONAL FINANCIAL CONSULTANT KIT** shows how to make money as an international financial consultant working with large lenders who finance big projects. Gives the agreements and forms needed, fee schedule, lender who might work with you, sample ads, sample letters, plus much more. With this kit on hand, the beginner can start seeking large deals using overseas funding sources. The kit provides a variety of lenders for international deals in all parts of the world. $100; 200 pages; 8½ × 11 in.

K-24 ***OFFSHORE BANKING KIT*** shows the reader how to form an offshore bank to receive deposits, make loans, handle credit cards, issue certificates of deposit, send money bank-to-bank, plus much more. Forming an offshore bank may be the answer to *your* funding needs because you will receive funds to invest. You will become a banker when you use the information in this kit. But it will take time and energy to get your offshore bank started. This kit tells you how and helps you get started sooner. $100; 200 pages; 8½ × 11 in.

ORDER FORM

Dear Ty: Please rush me the following:

☐ IWS-1	*Business Capital Sources*	$15.00	_____
☐ IWS-2	*Small Business Investment*	15.00	_____
☐ IWS-3	*World-wide Riches Vol. 1*	25.00	_____
☐ IWS-4	*World-wide Riches Vol. 2*	25.00	_____
☐ IWS-5	*How to Prepare Export-Import*	25.00	_____
☐ IWS-6	*Real Estate Riches Supplement*	15.00	_____
☐ IWS-7	*Radical New Road*	15.00	_____
☐ IWS-8	*60-Day Fully Financed*	29.50	_____
☐ IWS-9	*Credits and Collection*	29.50	_____
☐ IWS-10	*Mideast Banks*	15.00	_____
☐ IWS-11	*Export Mail-Order*	17.50	_____
☐ IWS-12	*Product Export Riches*	21.50	_____
☐ IWS-13	*Dir. of High-Discount*	17.50	_____
☐ IWS-14	*How to Finance Real Estate*	21.50	_____
☐ IWS-15	*Dir. of Freight Forwarders*	17.50	_____
☐ IWS-16	*Can You Afford Not to Be . . . ?*	10.00	_____
☐ IWS-17	*How to Find Hidden Wealth*	17.50	_____
☐ IWS-18	*How to Create Real Estate Fortune*	17.50	_____
☐ IWS-19	*Real Estate Second Mortgages*	17.50	_____
☐ IWS-20	*Guide to Business and Real Estate*	25.00	_____
☐ IWS-21	*Dir. of 2,500 Active Real Estate*		
	Lenders	25.00	_____
☐ IWS-22	*Ideas for Finding Capital*	24.50	_____
☐ IWS-23	*How to Become Wealthy Pub.*	17.50	_____
☐ IWS-24	*National Dir. Manufacturers' Reps*	28.80	_____
☐ IWS-25	*Business Plan Kit*	29.50	_____
☐ IWS-26	*Money Raiser's Dir. of*		
	Bank Credit Card Programs	19.95	_____
☐ IWS-27	*Global Cosigners and*		
	Money Finders Assoc.	50.00	_____
☐ IWS-28	*Wall Street Syndicators*	15.00	_____
☐ IWS-29	*Comprehensive Loan Sources for*		
	Business and Real Estate Loans	25.00	_____
☐ IWS-30	*Diversified Loan Sources for*		
	Business and Real Estate Loans	25.00	_____
☐ IWS-31	*Credit Power Reports*		
	Report No. 1	19.95	_____
	Report No. 2	19.95	_____
	Report No. 3	19.95	_____
	Report No. 4	19.95	_____
	Report No. 5	19.95	_____
☐ IWS-32	*Guaranteed Monthly Income*	15.00	_____
☐ IWSN-1	*International Wealth Success*	24.00	_____
☐ IWSN-2	*Money Watch Bulletin*	95.00	_____
☐ K-1	*Financial Broker*	99.50	_____
☐ K-2	*Starting Millionaire*	99.50	_____
☐ K-3	*Franchise Riches*	99.50	_____
☐ K-4	*Mail Order Riches*	99.50	_____
☐ K-5	*Zero Cash Success*	99.50	_____
☐ K-6	*Real Estate Riches*	99.50	_____
☐ K-7	*Business Borrowers*	99.50	_____
☐ K-8	*Raising Money from Grants*	99.50	_____
☐ K-9	*Fast Financing of Real Estate*	99.50	_____
☐ K-10	*Loans by Phone Kit*	100.00	_____

Order form is continued on back of this page

☐ K-11	*Loans by Mail Kit*	$100.00	_____
☐ K-12	*Real Estate Loan Getters Service Kit*	100.00	_____
☐ K-13	*Cash Credit Riches System Kit*	100.00	_____
☐ K-14	*Professional Practice Builders Kit*	100.00	_____
☐ K-15	*Venture Capital Millions Kit*	100.00	_____
☐ K-16	*Guaranteed Loan Money*	100.00	_____
☐ K-17	*Import-Export Riches Kit*	99.50	_____
☐ K-18	*Phone-in/Mail-in Grants Kit*	100.00	_____
☐ K-19	*Mega Money Methods*	100.00	_____
☐ K-20	*Foreclosures and Other Distressed Property Sales*	51.95	_____
☐ K-21	*Small Business Loan Program*	100.00	_____
☐ K-22	*Phone-in Mini-Lease Program*	100.00	_____
☐ K-23	*International Financial Consultant Kit*	100.00	_____
☐ K-24	*Offshore Banking Kit*	100.00	_____

Total Amount of Order _____

I am paying by: ☐ Check   ☐ MO/Cashier's Check   ☐ Visa/MC

Name: _____

Address: _____

City: _____ State: _____ Zip: _____

Visa/MC#: _____ Exp: _____

Signature: _____

Send all orders to: Tyler Hicks, Prima Publishing and Communications
P.O. Box 1260 HD, Rocklin CA 95677

Or with Visa/MC, call orders at (916) 624-5718 Mon.–Fri. 9 AM–4 PM PST

INDEX

acquisition, defined, 67
action planning, 99–116
  keys to, 99
  steps in, 101–102
advertisements, 91
  expanding, 67
  for loans, 85
  for money to loan, 86
  for real estate, 103
  successful, 158–162
advertising copywriters, hiring, 156–159, 161
airport greeter, making money as an, 90–91
American Booksellers Association, 233
attorneys,
  business plans and, 22
  corporate charters and, 235
  and licensing laws, 153
  and limited partnerships, 23
  offshore banking and, 194
  for real estate, 103
  and REITs, 211
  stock sales and, 21, 22
  and venture-capital funds, 213

bankruptcy, 147
banks,
  as asset-based lenders, 191
  offshore, 193–194
Beginning Wealth Builders (BWBs), 32
  basic drives in, 10–11
  business plans and, 30
  loans for, 15
benefit plans, 134–135
Better Business Bureau (BBB), 133–134, 155, 233
Breakout Financing, defined, 186
brokerage house, typical letter to, 180
brokers. *See* financial brokers
building conversion, making money from, 89
business buyer's comparison chart, 63

Business Capital Sources, 17
business development companies, 16–17, 110–112
business equipment, 229–230
businesses,
  buying, 13–14
  common problems in, 234–235
  expanding, 66–68
  loans for, 14–20
  money-making, 87–88
  owning, 4–5, 12–13, 61–71
  strong growth, 182–183
Business Plan Kit, 19, 22
business plans, 22, 29–45, 170
  action steps in, 101–102
  applying, 45–47
  descriptive, 39–40
  Executive Summary in, 33–37
  funding and, 40–41
  importance of, 29–31
  income and expense projections in, 41–45
  for real estate, 46
business startup, steps to, 102
bus tours, making money from, 140

Comprehensive Loan Sources, 110
corporate stocks and bonds, 21–23, 232
corporate umbrella, 106–107
cosigners,
  finding services, 149–150
  and guarantors, 149–151
credit bureaus, 105, 147–148
credit consulting, making money from, 93
Credits and Collection Kit, 88
credit unions, loans from, 190
customer service, 122–126
  building loyalty through, 125–126
  correcting errors in, 125
  examples of, 124
Customer Wants List, 123

Department of Housing and Urban Development (HUD), 208

direct response, 46, 59
  Executive Summary for, 36–37
  legal aspects of, 155
Discount Mortgage Broker's Cashout Kit, 84
diversifying, defined, 67

economic development offices, 152
employees, 128–129
entertainment businesses, 61
equity capital, 15, 20–25
equity kickers, defined, 59
excess funds, investing, 232
Executive Summary, 33–39, 57, 101–105
Export-Import Kit, 202

Federal Trade Commission (FTC), 155
financial brokers, 19, 45
  unlicensed, 153
financing, understanding, 14–16
first mortgage loans, making money from, 140–141
fix-up property, finding, 208
Foreclosure Kit, 107
4 Doctor Loan Programs, 86
franchise companies, 69

garden apartments, making money from, 89–90
general partner, defined, 23
Global Cosigners and Money Finders Association, 150
goals,
  acting on, 116–117
  enjoying, 54–55
  importance of, 4–5
  income, 8–9
  money making, 55–56
  steps to achieving, 168–169
  visualizing, 52–55
grants, 115
  getting, 20, 24–25
  "Phone-In/Mail-In" technique for, 24–25
  roadblocks to getting, 184–185
  successful, 185
guarantor organizations, 150–151

"hard money" lenders, defined, 187
health clubs, making money from, 140
health professionals,

getting loans for, 85–86
  making money from, 240–242
hiring practices, unique, 227
hobbies, as businesses, 5–8, 11–12
how-to-books, 91–92
How to Finance Real Estate Investments, 108
How to Get Rich, 8
How to Make a Fortune as a Licensing Agent, 137

import-export, 46, 59
  advantages of, 135–137, 138–139
  costs, 43–44
  Executive Summary, 36–37
  financing, 201–202
  income, 42–43
  marketing, 139
  profits, 45
  as a second business, 201–202
Import-Export Kit, 135, 136
income, estimating, 8–9, 41–45
income sources,
  controlling, 59–64
  finding, 62–64
income statement, typical store, 205
industry associations, joining, 232–234
Internal Revenue Service (IRS), 156
International Financial Consultant Kit, 234
International Wealth Success, 16, 33, 67, 111, 126, 160, 176, 188, 195
  newsletter, 18, 62, 155, 189, 202
invention marketing, 70
investing, in other businesses, 234–237
IWS, Inc., 76, 233
  loans from, 37–39, 225–226, 234–237

job development agencies, hiring through, 94, 227–228

lease broker,
  defined, 82–83
  making money as a, 141
legal and accounting advice, 155–156
lenders, rules for, 237–238
licensing business, 137

licensing law, 152–153
limited partnerships, 57
  corporations vs., 23
  selling shares in, 20–23
loan packagers, 69–70
loan rejections, dealing with,
  148–149
loans,
  acceptable purposes for, 19–20
  accounts receivable, 85, 86–87
  active business, 37–39
  amortization, 85
  asset-based, 191–193
  bank, 16
  business, 14–20
  by mail, 114–115
  cosigners for, 149–151
  credit union, 190
  development company, 94–95
  from excess funds, 232–238
  government, 116
  guarantors for, 150–151
  "hard money," 187–188
  home equity, 19, 112–114
  keys to getting, 15–20, 60–61,
    191
  no-credit-check, 186–188
  overseas, 189–190
  preapproved, 103
  private, 188–189
  real estate, 16, 17, 37–39
  rules for making, 237–238
  SBA, 219, 226
  second business, 201–202, 219–221
  small and minority business,
    86–87
  sources for, 16–19, 225–226
  specialty, 238–240
  to other companies, 234–237
loan turn-downs, overcoming,
  147–149
long-term mortgages, 19

Mail Order Loan Success System, 140
mail order. *See* direct response;
  import-export
Mini-Lease Kit, 141
money,
  borrowing, 146
  private, 115
  and RMA, 80–95
  sources of, 56–59, 78–80,
    110–116, 140, 186
money-making businesses, 59,
  87–88

Money Watch Bulletin, 189
mortgage,
  cashout deals, 83–84
  funds, 59
  lenders, 17
mortgaging-out money, 90
municipal bonds, buying and holding, 232
mutual funds,
  forming, 210–212, 214–215
  load and no-load, 215

Newsletter Association, 233
newsletters, making money from,
  157–158
newspaper advertisements, 85, 86,
  91, 103
no-credit-check-lenders, 186–188
nonrepayable capital. *See* equity
  capital

1-hour film developing centers,
  making money from, 140
other people's money (OPM),
  controlling, 81–87
  finding, 81

Parade magazine, 92
people, as resources, 121–142
Phone-In / Mail-In Grants Kit, 25
planning, 99–116
  strategies, 157–158
  See also business plans
"Potential Problem Analysis," 162
private stock offerings, 21–22,
  115–116
profit, computing, 35–36
prospectus. *See* business plans
public stock offerings, 21–22, 170,
  177–182
publishing, making money from,
  91–92

real estate,
  action plans, 101–105
  business plans, 46
  buying, 58–59
  corporate umbrella in, 106–107
  equity kickers in, 59
  Executive Summary for, 36–37
  finding profitable, 107–108
  home equity loans for, 112–114
  improving, 207
  income, 106–107
  investors, 58

legal aspects of, 155–156
loans for, 16, 17, 236
mortgage cashout deals in,
    83–84
renting, 70
returns on, 58–59
as a second business, 201, 202
as a takeover business, 206–208
real estate corporations, forming,
    106–107
Real Estate Investment Trust
    (REIT), 210–212
real estate law, loopholes in, 153
Real Estate Loan Getters Kit, 108
regulators, dealing with, 129–132
repossessed properties, 230–231
results,
    controlling, 169–170
    getting specific, 167–168
    through venture capital,
        183–184
retail businesses, 59
roadblocks to success,
    defined, 145
    overcoming, 145–164
    specific, 163, 184–185

sale and leaseback of equipment,
    85
sales,
    estimating, 35–36
    visualization of, 69–70
*SBIC Directory and Small Business
    Handbook*, 17
second businesses,
    building, 199–221
    examples of, 200
    getting money for, 210–215
    keys to building, 201
    picking, 200–201
    zero-cash approach for, 219–221
"secure jobs," disadvantages of,
    12–13
Securities and Exchange Commis-
    sion (SEC), 115–116, 170
    prospectus outline, 171–176
self-employment. *See* businesses,
    owning
service businesses, 61, 69
    Executive Summary for, 36–37
sharing business wealth, 227–230
Small Business Administration
    (SBA), 17, 116, 151–152,
    219, 226

Small Business Investment
    Companies (SBICs), 17, 61
Small Business Loan Kit, 87
specialty lender, defined, 238–240
stock offerings. *See* private stock of-
    ferings; public stock offerings
strong growth businesses, examples
    of, 182–183

takeovers, 202–210
trade associations, 133
travel agencies, making money
    from, 140
"turn-ons" as businesses, 5–8,
    11–12

U. S. Government bonds, buying
    and holding, 232
U. S. Postal Service, 155
unsecured signature loans, 85
used car dealerships, making mon-
    ey from, 140

vacation service businesses,
    215–219
    advantages of, 216, 218
    steps to forming, 217–218
vending machines, making money
    from, 140
venture capital, 17, 36, 94
    keys to getting, 182–184
venture-capital funds, 57
    forming, 210–212, 407
    getting money for, 213
Venture Capital Millions Kit, 58, 221
Veterans Administration (VA), 208
visualizing success, 51–64

Wall Street Syndicators, 22
wealth, steps to, 63–71
workers,
    finding suitable, 64–66
    freelance, 65–66
    steps in hiring, 65
Worldwide Riches Opportunities, 12

"Yellow Pages," 91
    for brokerage houses, 22
    for nonprofit lenders, 61
    for venture capital, 57

zero-cash financing,
    for second businesses, 219–221
    in takeovers, 202–203, 206